4/04

# FOR REFERENCE

**Do Not Take From This Room**

# WORLD OF ANIMALS

# 10 MAMMALS

## MARSUPIALS

Kangaroos, Possums, Koala ...

# PAT MORRIS, AMY-JANE BEER

GROLIER

*Mexican mouse opossum (1); Central American woolly opossum (2); black-shouldered opossum (3).*

Library of Congress Cataloging-in-Publication Data

Morris, Pat.
    Mammals / [Pat Morris, Amy-Jane Beer, Erica Bower].
       p. cm. -- (World of animals)
    Contents: v. 1. Small carnivores -- v. 2. Large carnivores -- v. 3. Sea mammals -- v. 4.
Primates -- v. 5. Large herbivores -- v. 6. Ruminant (horned) herbivores -- v. 7. Rodents
1 -- v. 8. Rodents 2 and lagomorphs -- v. 9. Insectivores and bats -- v. 10. Marsupials.
    ISBN 0-7172-5742-8 (set : alk. paper) -- ISBN 0-7172-5743-6 (v.1 : alk. paper) -- ISBN
0-7172-5744-4 (v.2 : alk. paper) -- ISBN 0-7172-5745-2 (v.3 : alk. paper) -- ISBN
0-7172-5746-0 (v.4 : alk. paper) -- ISBN 0-7172-5747-9 (v.5 : alk. paper) -- ISBN
0-7172-5748-7 (v.6 : alk. paper) -- ISBN 0-7172-5749-5 (v.7 : alk. paper) -- ISBN
0-7172-5750-9 (v.8 : alk. paper) -- ISBN 0-7172-5751-7 (v.9 : alk. paper) -- ISBN
0-7172-5752-5 (v.10 : alk. paper)
    1. Mammals--Juvenile literature. [1. Mammals.] I. Beer, Amy-Jane. II. Bower, Erica.
III. Title. IV. World of animals (Danbury, Conn.)

QL706.2 .M675 2003
599--dc21

2002073860

Published 2003 by Grolier,
Danbury, CT 06816
A division of Scholastic Library Publishing

This edition published exclusively for the school
and library market

Planned and produced by
Andromeda Oxford Limited
11–13 The Vineyard,
Abingdon, Oxon OX14 3PX

www.andromeda.co.uk

Copyright © Andromeda Oxford Limited 2003

**Project Director:**     Graham Bateman
**Editors:**     Angela Davies, Penny Mathias
**Art Editor and Designer:**     Steve McCurdy
**Cartographic Editor:**     Tim Williams
**Editorial Assistants:**     Marian Dreier, Rita
                    Demetriou
**Picture Manager:**     Claire Turner
**Picture Researcher:**     Vickie Walters
**Production:**     Clive Sparling
**Researchers:**    Dr. Erica Bower, Rachael Brooks,
              Rachael Murton, Eleanor Thomas

**Origination:** Unifoto International, South Africa

**Printed in China**

Set ISBN 0-7172-5742-8

# About This Volume

**M**arsupials represent an alternative way of being a mammal. They are highly successful creatures found mostly in Australia and South America. They live up trees, down burrows, and in the water, and are found everywhere from tropical jungles to parched deserts, although none live in the sea. Some are extremely well adapted to challenging environments and can be quite numerous. Others, especially in Australia, are very rare and have lost out in competition with imported placental (Eutherian) mammals. One species, the Virginia opossum, has successfully colonized large parts of North America. Monotremes are yet another way of being mammalian. They lay eggs, a peculiar habit that is not shared by other mammals. They too are successful in their way, but are few in number and live only in Australasia.

# Contents

*Koalas are strong, steady climbers and more agile than their unhurried movements suggest.*

*Some kangaroos and wallabies: rufous rat kangaroo (1); banded hare wallaby (2); quokka (3); burrowing bettong (4); yellow-footed rock wallaby (5).*

# How to Use This Set

*World of Animals: Mammals* is a 10-volume set that describes in detail mammals from all corners of the earth. Each volume brings together those animals that are most closely related and have similar lifestyles. So all the meat-eating groups (carnivores) are in Volumes 1 and 2, and all the seals, whales, and dolphins (sea mammals) are in Volume 3, and so on. To help you find volumes that interest you, look at pages 6 to 7 (Find the Animal). A brief introduction to each volume is also given on page 2 (About This Volume).

## Data panel presents basic statistics of each animal

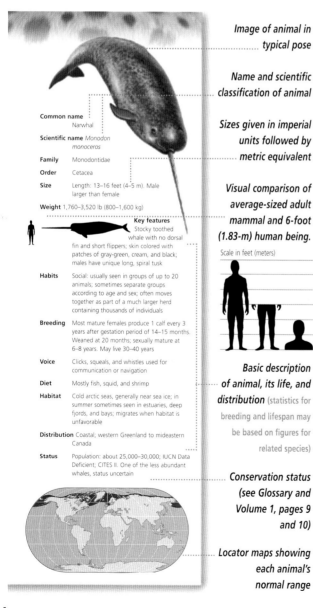

*Image of animal in typical pose*

*Name and scientific classification of animal*

**Common name**
Narwhal

**Scientific name** *Monodon monoceros*

**Family** Monodontidae

**Order** Cetacea

**Size** Length: 13–16 feet (4–5 m). Male larger than female

**Weight** 1,760–3,520 lb (800–1,600 kg)

**Key features** Stocky toothed whale with no dorsal fin and short flippers; skin colored with patches of gray-green, cream, and black; males have unique long, spiral tusk

**Habits** Social: usually seen in groups of up to 20 animals; sometimes separate groups according to age and sex; often moves together as part of a much larger herd containing thousands of individuals

**Breeding** Most mature females produce 1 calf every 3 years after gestation period of 14–15 months. Weaned at 20 months; sexually mature at 6–8 years. May live 30–40 years

**Voice** Clicks, squeals, and whistles used for communication or navigation

**Diet** Mostly fish, squid, and shrimp

**Habitat** Cold arctic seas, generally near sea ice; in summer sometimes seen in estuaries, deep fjords, and bays; migrates when habitat is unfavorable

**Distribution** Coastal; western Greenland to mideastern Canada

**Status** Population: about 25,000–30,000; IUCN Data Deficient; CITES II. One of the less abundant whales, status uncertain

*Sizes given in imperial units followed by metric equivalent*

*Visual comparison of average-sized adult mammal and 6-foot (1.83-m) human being.*

Scale in feet (meters)

| | |
|---|---|
| | 6 (1.83) |
| | 5 (1.5) |
| | 4 (1.2) |
| | 3 (0.9) |
| | 2 (0.6) |
| | 1 (0.3) |

*Basic description of animal, its life, and distribution* (statistics for breeding and lifespan may be based on figures for related species)

*Conservation status (see Glossary and Volume 1, pages 9 and 10)*

*Locator maps showing each animal's normal range*

## Article Styles

Articles are of three kinds. There are two types of introductory or review article: One introduces large animal groups like orders (such as whales and dolphins). Another introduces smaller groups like families (The Raccoon Family, for example). The articles review the full variety of animals to be found in different groups. The third type of article makes up most of each volume. It concentrates on describing individual animals typical of the group in great detail, such as the tiger. Each article starts with a fact-filled **data panel** to help you gather information at-a-glance. Used together, the three article styles enable you to become familiar with specific animals in the context of their evolutionary history and biological relationships.

## Article describes a particular animal

*Scientific name of animal*

*Common name of animal*

*Captions to photographs provide additional information about each animal's lifestyle*

LARGE CARNIVORES *Panthera tigris*

# Tiger

The tiger, with its black-and-orange striped coat, is one of the most distinctive of all mammals. It is feared the world over, but nowadays the species is severely reduced in numbers.

IN MANY WAYS THE TIGER IS MORE deserving of the title King of Beasts than its close cousin, the lion. It is the largest of all the cats, and its range once extended from the fringes of Europe eastward to Russia's Sea of Okhotsk and south to the Indonesian islands of Java and Bali. Tigers from different parts of this vast range differ considerably, so the species has been divided into eight subspecies. They are named after the region in which they occur, but most can also be distinguished by their appearance. For example, Siberian tigers are consistently bigger than other subspecies, with males weighing up to 660 pounds (300 kg). This almost certainly makes them the biggest cats ever to have lived, including huge extinct species such as the saber-toothed tiger and the cave lion.

**Common name** Tiger

**Scientific name** *Panthera tigris*

**Family** Felidae

**Order** Carnivora

**Size** Length head/body: 4.6–9 ft (1.4–2.7 m); tail length: 23–43 in (60–110 cm); height at shoulder: 31–43 in (80–110 cm)

**Weight** Male 200–660 lb (90–300 kg); female 143–364 lb (65–165 kg)

**Key features** Large, muscular cat with large head and long tail; unmistakable orange coat with dark stripes; underside white

**Habits** Solitary and highly territorial; active mostly at night; climbs and swims well

**Breeding** Litters of 1–6 (usually 2 or 3) cubs born at any time of year after gestation period of 95–110 days. Weaned at 3–6 months; females sexually mature at 3–4 years, males at 4–5 years. May live up to 26 years in captivity, rarely more than 10 in the wild

**Voice** Purrs, grunts, and blood-curdling roars

**Diet** Mainly large, hoofed mammals, including deer, buffalo, antelope, and gaur

**Habitat** Tropical forests and swamps, grasslands with good vegetation cover and water nearby

**Distribution** India, Bhutan, Bangladesh, Nepal, China, southeastern Siberia, Myanmar (Burma), Vietnam, Laos, Thailand, and Sumatra

**Status** Population: 5,000–7,500; IUCN Endangered; CITES I. Previously hunted for fur and body parts, and to protect people and livestock

*A Bengal tiger wades through water. Tigers are proficient swimmers and can cross rivers that are 4 to 5 miles (7 to 8 km) wide without difficulty.*

*Juvenile tigers are fond of play fighting, like the two below.*

## Different Adaptations

The smallest tigers came from Bali and rarely exceeded 220 pounds (100 kg) in weight. They are now probably extinct. As a general rule, body size relates to the climate and the type of prey available in different parts of the tiger's range. Siberian tigers need to cope with intensely cold and snowy winters, and specialize in catching large prey such as cattle and deer. In contrast, tigers in Indonesia inhabit tropical jungle where overheating is a serious problem for large animals, and the favored prey includes pigs and small deer. The Chinese tiger is thought to be the ancestor of the other types. Fossils show that tigers first appeared in China about 2 million years ago, and they spread north, south, and west from there. Modern Chinese tigers have several traits that zoologists consider rather primitive, including a shortened skull and relatively close-set eyes.

20 **SEE ALSO** Lion 2:14; Boar, Wild 5:76; Deer and Relatives 6:10

*Cross-references to relevant pages in this and other volumes*

*Easy-to-read and comprehensive text*

A number of other features help you navigate through the volumes and present you with helpful extra information. At the bottom of many pages are **cross-references** to other articles of interest. They may be to related animals, animals that live in similar places, animals with similar behavior, predators (or prey), and much more. Each volume also contains a **Set Index** to the complete *World of Animals: Mammals*. All animals mentioned in the text are indexed by common and scientific names, and many topics are also covered. A **Glossary** will also help you if there are words used in the text that you do not fully understand. Each volume ends with a list of useful **Further Reading and Websites** that help you take your research further. Finally, under the heading "List of Species" you will find expanded listings of the animals that are covered in each volume.

Introductory article describes family or closely related groups

SMALL CARNIVORES

# The Raccoon Family

*Detailed maps clarify animal's distribution*

*At-a-glance boxes cover topics of special interest*

*Meticulous drawings illustrate a typical selection of group members*

*Tables summarize classification of groups and give scientific names of animals mentioned in the text*

*Who's Who tables summarize classification of each major group and give scientific names of animals mentioned in the text*

The Disappearing Tiger

Introductory article describes major groups of animals

# WHALES AND DOLPHINS

*Graphic full-color photographs bring text to life*

*Detailed diagrams illustrate text*

# Find the Animal

**W**orld of Animals: Mammals is the first part of a library that describes all groups of living animals. Each cluster of volumes in World of Animals will cover a familiar group of animals—mammals, birds, reptiles and amphibians, fish, and insects and other invertebrates. These groups also represent categories of animals recognized by scientists (see The Animal Kingdom below).

## The Animal Kingdom

The living world is divided into five kingdoms, one of which (kingdom Animalia) is the main subject of the

World of Animals. Also included are those members of the kingdom Protista that were once regarded as animals, but now form part of a group that includes all single-cell organisms. Kingdom Animalia is divided into numerous major groups called Phyla, but only one of them (Chordata) contains those animals that have a backbone. Chordates, or vertebrates as they are popularly known, include all the animals familiar to us and those most studied by scientists—mammals, birds, reptiles, amphibians, and fish. In all, there are about 38,000 species of vertebrates, while the Phyla that contain animals without backbones (so-called invertebrates, such as insects, spiders, and so on) include at least 1 million species, probably many more. To find which set of volumes in the World of Animals is relevant to you, see the chart Main Groups of Animals (page 7).

Rodents (Order Rodentia): **squirrels, rats, mice Volume 7; cavies, porcupines, chinchillas Volume 8**

Lagomorphs (Order Lagomorpha): **rabbits, hares, pikas Volume 8**

Tree shrews (Order Scandentia): **Volume 9**

Insectivores (Order Insectivora): **shrews, moles, hedgehogs Volume 9**

Colugos, flying lemurs (Order Dermoptera): **Volume 8**

Primates (Order Primates): **lemurs, monkeys, apes Volume 4**

Pangolins (Order Pholidota): **Volume 9**

Carnivores (Order Carnivora): **raccoons, weasels, otters, skunks Volume 1; cats, dogs, bears, hyenas Volume 2**

Seals and sea lions (Order Pinnipedia): **Volume 3**

Odd-toed ungulates (Order Perissodactyla): **horses, rhinoceroses, tapirs Volume 5**

Even-toed ungulates (Order Artiodactyla): **pigs, camels Volume 5; deer, cattle, sheep, goats Volume 6**

Whales and dolphins (Order Cetacea): **Volume 3**

Bats (Order Chiroptera): **Volume 9**

Xenarthrans (Order Xenarthra): **anteaters, sloths, armadillos Volume 9**

Elephant shrews (Order Macroscelidea): **Volume 9**

Aardvark (Order Tubulidentata): **Volume 9**

Hyraxes (Order Hyracoidea): **Volume 8**

Dugongs, manatees (Order Sirenia): **Volume 3**

Elephants (Order Proboscidea): **Volume 5**

Marsupials: **opposums, kangaroos, koala Volume 10**

Monotremes (Order Monotremata): **platypus, echidnas Volume 10**

## Mammals in Particular

World of Animals: Mammals focuses on the most familiar of animals, those most easily recognized as having fur (although this may be absent in many sea mammals like whales and dolphins), and that provide milk for their young. Mammals are divided into major groups (carnivores, primates, rodents, and marsupials to name just

*The chart shows the major groups of mammals in this set arranged in evolutionary relationship (see page 10). The volume in which each group appears is indicated. You can find individual entries by looking at the contents page for each volume or by consulting the set index.*

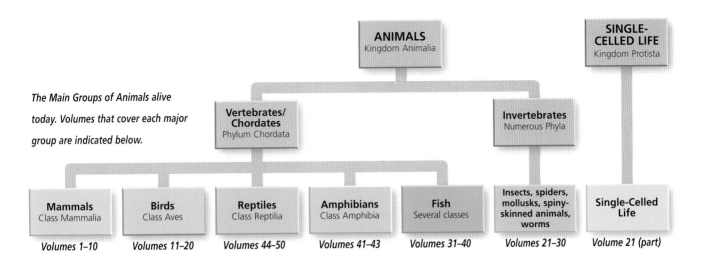

| ANIMALS Kingdom Animalia | | | | | | SINGLE-CELLED LIFE Kingdom Protista |

| Vertebrates/ Chordates Phylum Chordata | | | | | Invertebrates Numerous Phyla | |

| Mammals Class Mammalia | Birds Class Aves | Reptiles Class Reptilia | Amphibians Class Amphibia | Fish Several classes | Insects, spiders, mollusks, spiny-skinned animals, worms | Single-Celled Life |
| Volumes 1–10 | Volumes 11–20 | Volumes 44–50 | Volumes 41–43 | Volumes 31–40 | Volumes 21–30 | Volume 21 (part) |

a few). All the major groups are shown on the chart on page 6. To help you find particular animals, a few familiar ones, such as sheep, goats, cats, and dogs, have been included in the chart.

## Naming Mammals

To be able to discuss animals, names are needed for the different kinds. Most people regard tigers as one kind of animal and lions as another. All tigers look more or less alike. They breed together and produce young like themselves. This popular distinction between kinds of animals corresponds closely to the zoologists' distinction between species. All tigers belong to one species and all lions to another. The lion species has different names in different languages (for example, *Löwe* in German, *Simba* in Swahili), and often a single species may have several common names. For example, the North American mountain lion is also known as the cougar, puma, panther, and catamount.

Zoologists find it convenient to have internationally recognized names for species and use a standardized system of two-word Latinized names. The lion is called *Panthera leo* and the tiger *Panthera tigris*. The first word, *Panthera*, is the name of the genus (a group of closely similar species), which includes the lion and the tiger. The second word, *leo* or *tigris*, indicates the particular species within the genus. Scientific names are recognized all over the world. The scientific name is used whatever the language, even where the alphabet is different, as in Chinese or Russian. The convention allows for precision and helps avoid most confusion. However, it is also common for one species to apparently have more than one scientific name. That can be because a particular

species may have been described and named at different times without the zoologists realizing it was one species.

It is often necessary to make statements about larger groups of animals: for example, all the catlike animals or all the mammals. A formal system of classification makes this possible. Domestic cats are similar to lions and tigers, but not as similar as those species are to each other (for example, they do not roar). They are put in a different genus (*Felis*), but *Felis*, *Panthera*, and other catlike animals are grouped together as the family Felidae. The flesh-eating mammals (cats, dogs, hyenas, weasels, and so on), together with a few plant-eaters that are obviously related to them (such as pandas), are grouped in the order Carnivora. These and all the other animals that suckle their young are grouped in the class Mammalia. Finally, the mammals are included, with all other animals that have backbones (fish, amphibians, reptiles, and birds) and some other animals that seem to be related to them, in the Phylum Chordata.

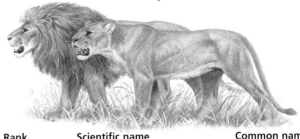

| Rank | Scientific name | Common name |
|---|---|---|
| Phylum | Chordata | Animals with a backbone |
| Class | Mammalia | All mammals |
| Order | Carnivora | Flesh-eaters/carnivores |
| Family | Felidae | All cats |
| Genus | *Panthera* | Big cats |
| Species | *leo* | Lion |

*The kingdom Animalia is subdivided into phylum, classes, orders, families, genera, and species. Above is the classification of the lion.*

# MARSUPIALS

**M**arsupials are a diverse group of mammals that are united by a highly distinctive method of reproduction. Newborn marsupials are tiny, entering the world in an undeveloped, virtually embryonic state. The majority of their development takes place outside the mother's body during an extended period of suckling—usually in a pouch on the mother's abdomen. By contrast, in nonmarsupial or "placental" mammals most development occurs in the mother's womb. In most other ways the marsupials are fairly typical mammals.

## Many Types of Marsupial

Because the group is defined by breeding biology rather than by obvious physical characteristics, it is difficult to describe a "typical" marsupial. The basic marsupial body plan is highly adaptable, as can be seen in the extraordinary diversity of shapes, sizes, and lifestyles adopted by the 300 or so living species. However, today's marsupials represent only a fraction of the diversity that existed in the past.

Anatomically speaking, the most important difference between marsupials and placental mammals is the structure of their reproductive organs. In a female marsupial each of the two ovaries releases eggs into a separate uterus. In placental mammals there is just one central uterus.

Female marsupials also have two vaginas through which the male's sperm must pass in order to fertilize the eggs. The males of many marsupial species have a forked penis to help deliver sperm to both uteri. When the time comes for the young marsupial to be born, a third opening develops: This birth canal is similar to the single vagina of placental mammals. In kangaroos and the honey possum it is a permanent structure after the first birth, but in all other marsupials it seals over after each litter is born.

The skeleton of marsupials also shows some adaptations to their unique mode of reproduction, including additional bones attached to the pelvis. The extra bones help support the weight of infant marsupials

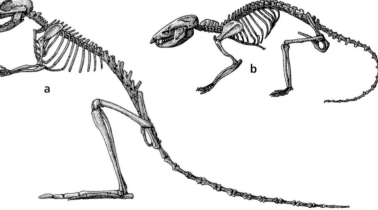

⬆ *Skeletons of the Tasmanian bettong (a) and Virginia opossum (b). The Tasmanian bettong has small forelimbs and large hind limbs for leaping. Its stance is almost completely upright, and the tail is long and used as an extra prop or foot. The Virginia opossum is medium sized, with unspecialized features shared with its marsupial ancestors. The skull and teeth are those of a generalist, and the tail is long and prehensile, acting as a "fifth hand." The hind limbs are only slightly longer than the forelimbs.*

↑ *The eastern barred bandicoot is virtually extinct on the Australian mainland. The species' survival depends on a reintroduction program whereby captive-bred animals are released into protected sites.*

while they are attached to the female's teats or carried in her pouch. However, these so-called "epipubic bones" are also present in male marsupials and monotremes (only some of which have pouches) and in reptiles, which do not suckle or carry their young.

## Placental versus Marsupial Mammals

Physiologically, marsupials show a number of differences from placental mammals. In general, they have a slightly lower (but still closely controlled) body temperature, and their metabolism ticks over at a slightly slower rate. As a result, it takes less energy to maintain a marsupial body than that of a placental mammal of the same weight. Marsupials are therefore better off than placental

## Who's Who among the Marsupials?

Infraclass Metatheria

**ORDER:** Didelphimorphia—American opossums: 63 species in 1 family

**Family:** Didelphidae, divided into 2 subfamilies

   **Subfamily:** Didelphinae—58 species in 12 genera, including water opossum (*Chironectes minimus*); Virginia opossum (*Didelphis virginiana*)

   **Subfamily:** Caluromyinae—5 species in 3 genera, including black-shouldered opossum (*Caluromysiops irrupta*)

**ORDER:** Paucituberculata—shrew or rat opossums: 5 species in 1 family

**Family:** Caenolestidae—3 genera, including gray-bellied shrew opossum (*Caenolestes caniventer*); Chilean shrew opossum (*Rhyncholestes raphanurus*)

**ORDER:** Microbiotheria—1 species in 1 family

**Family:** Microbiotheriidae, monito del monte (*Dromiciops gliroides*)

**ORDER:** Dasyuromorphia—Australasian carnivorous marsupials: 64 species in 3 families

**Family:** Dasyuridae—62 species in 16 genera, including fawn antechinus (*Antechinus bellus*); hairy-footed dunnart (*Sminthopsis hirtipes*)

**Family:** Thylacinidae—1 species in 1 genus, thylacine (*Thylacinus cynocephalus*)

**Family:** Myrmecobiidae—1 species in 1 genus, numbat (*Myrmecobius fasciatus*)

**ORDER:** Peramelemorphia—bandicoots and bilbies: 21 species in 2 families

**Family:** Peramelidae—10 species in 4 genera, including long-nosed bandicoot (*Perameles nasuta*); eastern barred bandicoot (*P. gunnii*)

**Family:** Peroryctidae—11 species in 4 genera, including mouse bandicoot (*Microperoryctes murina*); Clara's echymipera (*Echymipera clara*)

**ORDER:** Notoryctemorphia—marsupial moles: 2 species in 1 family

**Family:** Notoryctidae, northwestern marsupial mole (*Notoryctes caurinus*); marsupial mole (*Notoryctes typhlops*)

**ORDER:** Diprotodontia—Australasian herbivorous marsupials: 125 species in 10 families

**Family:** Phalangeridae—cuscuses, brushtails, and true possums: 20 species in 6 genera, including mountain cuscus (*Phalanger carmelitae*); common brushtail possum (*Trichosurus vulpecula*)

**Family:** Pseudocheiridae—ringtails and other large possums: 15 species in 5 genera, including green ringtail possum (*Pseudochirops archeri*); plush-coated ringtail possum (*P. corinnae*)

**Family:** Petauridae—gliders and stiped possums: 11 species in 3 genera, including mahogany glider (*Petaurus gracilis*); striped possum (*Dactylopsila trivirgata*)

**Family:** Burramyidae—pygmy possums: 5 species in 2 genera, including eastern pygmy possum (*Cercartetus nanus*); mountain pygmy possum (*Burramys parvus*)

**Family:** Acrobatidae—feathertail possums: 2 species in 2 genera, pygmy or feathertail glider (*Acrobates pygmaeus*); feathertail possum (*Distoechurus pennatus*)

**Family:** Tarsipedidae—honey possum: 1 species in 1 genus (*Tarsipes rostratus*)

**Family:** Phascolarctidae—koala: 1 species in 1 genus (*Phascolarctos cinereus*)

**Family:** Vombatidae—wombats: 3 species in 2 genera, including common wombat (*Vombatus ursinus*)

**Family:** Hypsiprymnodontidae—musky rat kangaroo: 1 species in 1 genus (*Hypsiprymnodon moschatus*)

**Family:** Macropodidae—66 species in 3 subfamilies

   **Subfamily:** Sthenurinae—sthenurines: 1 species in 1 genus, banded hare wallaby (*Lagostrophus fasciatus*)

   **Subfamily:** Potoroinae—bettongs and potoroos: 9 species in 4 genera, including Tasmanian bettong (*Bettongia gaimardi*); long-nosed potoroo (*Potorous tridactylus*)

   **Subfamily:** Macropodinae—kangaroos and wallabies: 56 species in 10 genera, including red kangaroo (*Macropus rufus*); yellow-footed rock wallaby (*Petrogale xanthopus*)

mammals in an environment where food is hard to come by. But they cannot put on weight as fast as placental mammals and, as a rule, develop more slowly.

Ever since the first known marsupials (the opossums of South America) were discovered, the classification of the marsupial group has been subject to almost constant revision. The "early" species were placed in a new order—the Marsupialia. But problems arose from trying to squeeze such an amazingly diverse assortment of animals into one box. We now know that the marsupials are far too varied to belong in the same order. As a group, marsupials are on an equal footing with the placental mammals. Nevertheless, they are often treated as poor relations. The scientific name for placental mammals is Eutheria. Literally translated, it means "true mammals," implying that marsupials (scientific name Metatheria) are somehow inferior to placentals when in fact they just have a different way of being a mammal.

*An infant common brushtail possum attached to its mother's nipple in her pouch. It will be weaned at about six months.*

## Pouches

The word marsupial comes from the Latin meaning "pouch." In many species the young spend the suckling period protected from the outside world in a pouch of skin that encloses the teats on the mother's belly. However, the possession of a pouch is not foolproof evidence that an animal is a marsupial. As a rule, only female marsupials have a pouch; and while it may be well developed in some species, in others it is little more than a fold of skin. In some marsupials the pouch is temporary, only appearing when the female is ready to breed. In others it never develops at all. Nor is the development of a pouch for incubating young an exclusively marsupial characteristic. Female echidnas suckle their young in a pouch as well. Marsupial pouches come in a variety of shapes and sizes. The largest, best-developed pouches are found in species that hop (kangaroos), climb (koalas and possums), or burrow (wombats and bandicoots)—activities that would endanger exposed young. In upright species, such as kangaroos, the pouch opens at the front so that the youngster does not tumble out. In digging animals, such as bandicoots and marsupial moles, the pouch opens to the rear so that it does not fill with dirt. The young of pouchless marsupials are carried dangling from the mother's teats. In some species they are protected by a growth of thick belly hair. In others they simply hang on—even dragging on the ground as they grow bigger. At a later stage they may be left for a time in a den or burrow. Alternatively, they may take to riding on their mother's back.

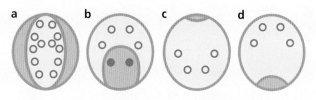

*Different pouch types (circles represent arrangement of nipples inside pouch): (a) is the most rudimentary version, with folds of skin on either side of the nipples; (b) is more pouchlike; deeper pouches (c) are used by climbers, leapers, or diggers; backward-opening pouches (d) are common to burrowers such as wombats.*

## Origins

Marsupials and eutherians (placental mammals) are sister groups. They come from the same ancestral stock, which probably diverged about 120 million years ago in the Cretaceous period. The earliest marsupials are likely to have been small- to medium-sized insectivorous mammals, not unlike modern bandicoots. Most evidence at present suggests that the first marsupials appeared in North America. The oldest known marsupial fossils are 75 to 100 million years old and come from river deposits in Utah and Alberta. From there the ancestors of today's marsupials dispersed into South America and eventually into Antarctica, Australia, and New Guinea. Dispersal to these areas was possible since, until the end of the Eocene period (40 million years ago), they were united as a single supercontinent known as Gondwanaland.

The first Australian marsupials were probably small, rather ratlike animals. They may have been similar to the monito del monte, a rare South American marsupial and the sole surviving member of the marsupial order Microbiotheria (see box). Unfortunately, Australia's fossil record is far from complete, and the first 30 to 40 million years of marsupial occupation are rather a mystery. By the mid-Miocene period, 20 million years ago, Australia was a densely forested continent with a rich marsupial fauna that was adapted to life in and among trees. However, climate change resulted in a steady decline in the lush vegetation cover. Today the forest-dwelling marsupials are restricted to northern and eastern Australia and New Guinea. Other marsupials moved with the times and became adapted to life in grassland, scrub, and desert.

## Marsupial Reproduction

Marsupials have the smallest babies and the shortest pregnancy of any mammals. Litters range in size from one to 56 young. Newborns of large species have the fastest growth rates: A young red kangaroo can increase its birthweight by more than 10,000 times in just 12 months. However, compared with the development of placental mammals (from conception to weaning), development in marsupials is exceedingly slow—18 weeks in the antechinus compared to just six in the brown rat.

# Gondwanaland—the Marsupial Kingdom

**120 million years ago (early Cretaceous period):** Americas are united, but have separated from Africa. South America is linked to Gondwana (southern supercontinent, also including Australia, New Zealand, Antarctica, and New Guinea). First marsupials appear.

**80 million years ago:** South America separates from North America, but remains closely associated at its southern tip with the united Antarctic–Australian supercontinent. Marsupials die out in North America, but thrive in Gondwana, where there is no competition from placental mammals.

**40 million years ago:** Continents drift apart; Australia, New Guinea, South America, and Antarctica separate. Marsupial populations on each become isolated. In South America marsupials evolve dramatically, resulting in animals as diverse as the fearsome borhyaenids (dominant predators, not unlike saber-toothed tigers), opossums, and tiny mouselike microbiotherians. Similar radiations probably happen in Australia and Antarctica.

**10 million years ago until the present:** South America reunites with North America. Placental mammals migrate into South America, and most families of marsupials die out, leaving just the opossums. Antarctic marsupials die out as climate becomes colder. Australian marsupials continue to thrive, adapting to drier conditions as Australia drifts north, and the climate gets warmer. Diversity of marsupials on New Guinea declines after separation from Australia, but land bridges during periods of low sea level allow some exchange of species. Arrival of humans (40,000 to 60,000 years ago) and placental carnivores leads to decline of some marsupial predators.

European settlement in 18th century triggers widespread declines among marsupial species in Australia.

120 mya

80 mya

40 mya

One of the advantages of marsupial-style reproduction is that the pregnancy needs relatively low levels of investment from the mother. This is in contrast to placental mammals, in which by the time a baby is born, the female has already devoted a considerable amount of time, energy, and metabolic resources to its growth and development. To lose a newborn baby (to a predator or because of a birth defect or sudden lack of food) is both costly and wasteful. It also leaves the mother with less energy for future breeding attempts.

For a marsupial mother, however, the main investment happens after birth, when the youngsters are attached to her teats and in need of a steady supply of milk. In the event of a drought, for example, or a youngster being born weak, a marsupial female can abandon the breeding attempt early on and start again at much less cost to herself.

## Embryonic Diapause

Some marsupials have taken their potential for rapid rebreeding to its extreme, with a phenomenon known as embryonic diapause. Like most other mammals, female marsupials can only conceive at a certain time in their estrous (reproductive) cycle. The cycle is normally halted during gestation because there is no reason for a female to mate when she is already pregnant. In many marsupials the period of gestation is so short that it does not disrupt the estrous cycle, and the female can come into breeding condition again soon after the birth of a litter.

Consequently, if anything happens to the first litter, the female is already pregnant with a replacement, and no time is wasted waiting to become fertile again or finding a mate. If, on the other hand, all is well with the first litter, the estrous cycle will stop after the second successful mating. As long as there are young attached to the female's teats and embryos in her uteri, she will not need to mate again. The second litter of embryos cannot be born while the first are still suckling, so they enter a state of suspended development inside the mother. In fact, each one develops no further than a ball of about 100 cells, called a blastocyst. These diapausing embryos only resume their development if the firstborn litter dies

⊕ *A baby spotted cuscus high in the trees in the forests of New Guinea. Spotted cuscuses mainly inhabit rainforest areas and are arboreal and nocturnal. Their diet consists of leaves, fruit, and flowers.*

or is almost ready to detach from the teats and leave the pouch. Diapause is maintained by the hormone prolactin, which is produced in response to suckling. The control is so precise that the reactivated embryos can be born within a day of the pouch being vacated by their elder siblings.

Because the young are born so small, births happen quickly and with minimum inconvenience to the mother. She will usually adopt a sitting position so that the cloaca faces forward, and the newborn can crawl directly up to the teats. The number of teats varies widely from two to 26. The body of a newborn marsupial is underdeveloped except for its front legs, which are disproportionately large and equipped with claws to help the baby clamber through the mother's fur. Once it finds a teat, it instinctively latches on. When the milk starts to flow, the teat swells up in the baby's mouth, preventing it from letting go. In many species the teats are sheltered within the mother's pouch, where her offspring are then nurtured. Usually the pouch faces forward, toward the mother's head, but in some species it faces backward. Many marsupials do not have a true pouch at all, and the babies develop among their mother's fur instead.

During the early stages of development the baby's digestive system is underdeveloped. The milk it receives is thin but contains plenty of easily absorbed sugars. As time goes by, the milk becomes richer, until in the final stages of suckling it is thick and fatty. In species like kangaroos, in which a female may have young from two litters suckling at the same time (one in the pouch and an older one following behind), she will produce two completely different kinds of milk from different teats so that each youngster has its own custom-made supply.

## Lifestyles

Marsupial feeding behavior is highly variable. The earliest marsupials were probably omnivores (animals that feed on both animal and vegetable substances). It is thought that they specialized mostly in insects. Modern marsupials make a living as leaf-eaters, grazers, insectivores, nectar-drinkers, sap-feeders, predators, scavengers, and omnivores. Some, such as the termite-eating numbat, are highly specialized, while others remain true generalists, like the Virginia opossum. Marsupials move by running, climbing, digging, hopping, and even gliding through the air. The vast majority of marsupials are at least partially nocturnal, and most species use scent and sound for communication in preference to visual signaling. Several species are strong swimmers, and one, the South American water opossum or yapok, spends much of its life in water. The otterlike yapok lives in a riverside burrow and does most of its foraging in the water. Females have a watertight pouch in which young are sealed during a dive. Unusually, the male yapok also has a pouch that encloses the scrotum when swimming, so making the animal more streamlined.

There is a commonly held perception that marsupials are not as smart as other mammals. Undeniably, most seem to have smaller brains than placental mammals of comparable size. History also shows that in competition with introduced placental animals marsupials rarely come out on top. However, most assessments of intelligence have so far been rather subjective. Left undisturbed in the right environment, a marsupial is just as capable of making the right survival decisions as any other mammal.

# American Opossums

For almost 300 years the American opossums were the only marsupials known to western science. They were "discovered" by Spanish explorers in South America (where they were already well known to the native people). Sixteenth-century zoologists interpreted the pouch in which female opossums suckled their young as a kind of external womb. They named the group the Didelphidae, meaning "two wombs"—one inside, one outside. The fact that female opossums—along with all other marsupials—actually have a double uterus was not discovered until later, making the name doubly fitting.

In those days marsupial reproduction seemed highly mysterious. Some early accounts even suggested that the tiny babies in the female opossum's pouch were born through the mother's nose. The theory sounds outrageous, but at the time it must have seemed plausible. It explained the male opossum's oddly forked penis, and the fact that minute babies appeared in the pouch after the female had spent some time with her face pushed into it. We now know that the penis is forked to deliver sperm to both vaginas and that the female licks her pouch clean when a litter is due.

## Origins

The story of American opossum ancestry goes back to the origin of all marsupials. The group evolved in North America during the Cretaceous period, about 120 million years ago. Some of these early marsupials subsequently made it across land bridges to Europe and from there to North Africa. Others ventured into South America before it separated from the north.

Exactly what happened to the early North American marsupials will never be known for sure, but many appear to have gone extinct about the same time as the dinosaurs. Others disappeared a little later, possibly as a result of competition with new placental mammals that were arriving by way of a land link with Asia. North American marsupials disappeared completely by the

**SEE ALSO** Carnivores, Small **1:**18; Carnivores, Large **2:**8; Primates **4:**8; Opossum, Virginia **10:**18

Miocene (15 to 20 million years ago), as did the few species that had colonized Europe and North Africa.

Meanwhile, the mammals of South America were enjoying a period of isolation that lasted 55 million years. During this time the resident marsupials diversified in size, shape, and lifestyle and rose to supremacy among the native fauna. However, their reign was cut short during the Pliocene (about 5 million years ago). A brief land link to North America allowed an influx of advanced, highly competitive placental mammals, including primates and

⊕ *A gray-bellied slender mouse opossum forages on the forest floor in Venezuela. The species is mainly nocturnal and—in common with most other mouse opossums—feeds primarily on insects and fruit.*

carnivores. The intruders rapidly displaced all the large marsupials and condemned them to extinction. It was not until a further 4 million years had passed that the two continents were again reunited, and North America was repopulated by just one representative of the marsupial group, the Virginia opossum.

**15**

### What Are American Opossums?

Opossums are small marsupials, none larger than a house cat and some less than 3 inches (7 cm) long. Most are proficient climbers with long tails, which in most species are prehensile and only partially furred. There are five toes on each foot, and the hallux (big toe) is opposable, allowing the opossum to grip branches with its hind feet. Opossums have a pointed face with long, sensitive whiskers, large, forward-facing eyes, and large, mobile ears. The females of some species have a pouch, while in others the young remain exposed throughout the suckling period. Opossums have a lot of teeth—up to 50 in many species. These are sharp and adapted for snapping up prey and crushing it, rather than shearing or grinding. Only one species, the Virginia opossum, lives in North America. The rest are Central and South American.

The majority of American marsupials belong in a single family (the Didelphidae) within the order Didelphimorphia. Didelphids come in a variety of shapes, sizes, and levels of specialization. They range from the common Virginia opossum—an opportunist that lives in many different habitats and eats all sorts of things—to the remarkable yapok, or water opossum, which hunts underwater. The large pouched opossums and the four-eyed opossums are generalists. They use excellent climbing skills to thoroughly explore their varied habitats and make the most of almost any feeding opportunity. The mouse opossums have a very long tail, which in some species thickens near the base during summer to store fat for winter. The short-tailed opossums are also small, mostly terrestrial, and favor live prey over other kinds of food. The woolly and black-shouldered opossums are larger and highly specialized for life in the trees. Along with the mouselike bushy-tailed opossum these species are placed in a subfamily called the Caluromyinae.

There are six other species of native American marsupial. Their evolutionary paths diverged so long ago that they are classified in orders outside the Didelphimorphia. Five of them, the so-called shrew opossums (Caenolestidae), are distinguished by having just one pair of incisor teeth in the lower jaw. The same "diprotodont" dentition evolved separately in a branch of Australian marsupials. The sixth non-didelphid species in South America—the unique monito del monte—is even more of an oddity (see box).

### Lifestyle

Most opossums live in forests and spend many hours in the trees, foraging, resting, and rearing young. Most will eat insects and small vertebrates, as well as plant material. Opossums do not defend territories, and their home ranges change throughout the year according to the available food resources. Each animal has several nests within its range, and they may be used by more than one animal at different times. Generally, individuals live alone and avoid company, except when looking for a mate. Aggression is common, especially when opossums meet around a shared food source. Courtship is minimal: Male opossums approach potential mates and are either ignored, driven away, or accepted, depending on the female's condition. Mating in some species is prolonged for several hours, increasing the male's chances of fathering a litter. The longest-lasting relationships are

## Monito del Monte—The Little Monkey of the Mountains

The monito del monte, the sole surviving member of the order Microbiotheria, is a mouselike, forest-dwelling marsupial from central Chile. It is the subject of much local superstition, but zoologists also find it fascinating. Certain anatomical characteristics distinguish the monito from all other marsupials in South America: The animal represents a very early offshoot from the main line of opossum evolution. In some ways (notably the structure of bones in the feet) the monito appears to be more closely related to Australian marsupials. Animals not unlike the monito may have been among the few that managed to cross from South America to Antarctica and Australia while the three continents were still closely associated over 60 million years ago. Hence the monito may be the only living example of the group from which today's Australian marsupial fauna arose.

between mothers and their offspring, but young tend to disperse soon after weaning. Opossums do not live for long, so it is in every animal's interest to find a suitable breeding area as soon as possible. Breeding is usually timed so that young are weaned during the most productive season.

## Where Opossums Live

American opossums can be found throughout most of South America, and one species—the Virginia opossum—occurs naturally in the eastern United States and southeastern Canada; it has been introduced to the West Coast and continues to spread north, south, and east. Most opossums live in wooded habitats or places where there are suitable daytime hideaways. The excellent climbing skills of many species allow them to fully exploit a three-dimensional vegetated habitat, foraging anywhere from ground level to 80 feet (25 m) up in the tree canopy.

*⊕ Some representative American opossum species: Central American woolly opossum resting in a tree (1); black-shouldered opossum using its prehensile tail for balance as it climbs down a branch (2); Mexican mouse opossum foraging for fruit (3); gray four-eyed opossum eating an insect grub (4); water opossum, or yapok, with its distinctive webbed feet (5).*

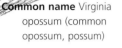

**Common name** Virginia opossum (common opossum, possum)

**Scientific name** *Didelphis virginiana*

**Family** Didelphidae

**Order** Didelphimorphia

**Size** Length head/body: 14–22 in (35–55 cm); tail length: 10–21 in (25–54 cm)

**Weight** 4.5–12 lb (2–5.5 kg)

**Key features** Cat-sized animal with short legs and long, naked tail; pointed snout, large black eyes, and round, naked ears; white-tipped guard hairs make coat appear shaggy; hind feet have opposable first toe; female has up to 15 teats in well-developed pouch

**Habits** Mostly active at night; solitary; swims and climbs well

**Breeding** Up to 56 (usually about 21) young born after gestation period of 13 days. Young emerge from pouch at 70 days. Weaned at 3–4 months; sexually mature at 6–8 months. May live up to 5 years in captivity, 3 in the wild

**Voice** Clicking sounds; also growls, hisses, and screeches when angry

**Diet** Small animals, including reptiles, mammals, and birds; invertebrates such as insects; plant material, including fruit and leaves; carrion; human refuse

**Habitat** Wooded areas or scrub, usually near watercourses or close to swamps

**Distribution** Eastern and central U.S.; West Coast south through Central America to Nicaragua

**Status** Population: abundant. Widespread; increasing in numbers and range

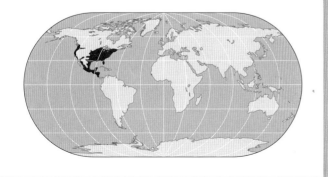

# Virginia Opossum

*Didelphis virginiana*

*As North America's only native marsupial, the Virginia opossum is worthy of attention. However, there is far more to the species than mere geographical novelty.*

THE VIRGINIA OPOSSUM IS ONE of the world's great mammalian success stories. Its ability to thrive—even where humans have made significant changes in its natural habitat—has earned it popular recognition and respect. Unlike many other marsupials, it is even known to thrive in the face of direct competition from placental mammals. Indeed, the Virginia opossum's adaptability clearly demonstrates that marsupials are not inferior to placental mammals as is sometimes implied. Opossums may lack the kind of intelligence generally attributed to monkeys or dogs, but the species compares favorably with other small- to medium-sized generalist mammals.

## Disheveled Appearance

The Virginia opossum is larger than most other members of its family. It has a rather untidy, disheveled appearance owing to the long, white-tipped guard hairs that emerge beyond its soft underfur. The underfur varies from dense and woolly in the north to thin and sparse in the warmer south.

The general scruffiness of the Virginia opossum is not helped by the fact that the long tail is naked for much of its length and often damaged by frostbite, as are the ears. However, far from being just an unsightly appendage, the tail is invaluable in climbing, being fully prehensile (able to grip). Serving as a fifth limb, it can grasp branches so effectively that the opossum is able to dangle by its tail alone. The tail is also used for carrying bedding materials to the nest: The opossum scrapes leaves and grass together with its paws and then grasps the vegetation with its tail for transportation.

 **SEE ALSO** Mouse, House **7:**68; Opossums, American **10:**14

The Virginia opossum's feet are also highly dexterous and can grip and manipulate objects while feeding. All four feet have five toes with strong, sharp claws, except for the first toe of each hind foot, which is clawless and opposable (used like a thumb for gripping).

## Healthy Appetite

Nowhere is the opossum's flexibility and generalist way of life better illustrated than in its diet. It will eat almost anything from mice, birds, and rabbits to beetles, snails, and seeds. The occasional frog or other amphibian is even known to appear on the menu. The Virginia opossum has learned the art of raiding trashcans in gardens and at picnic sites, and will happily devour food left out for birds or a pet dog. In the north of its range it takes advantage of the abundant food supplies in the summer months, often becoming very fat.

The Virginia opossum does not store food for winter, so its fat reserves can be vital in helping see it through the cold season. Even so, the animals still need to forage all year round, and they do not hibernate. Foraging generally happens at night. However, in winter the opossum may emerge more often during the day, and sometimes basks in the sun as an energy-efficient way of keeping warm.

Opossums may travel distances of up to 1.8 miles (3 km) a night in search of food, moving along the ground and through trees. They are often at least partially nomadic, occupying home ranges that cover 12 to 600 acres (5 to 240 ha). The same home range is used continuously for a period of months or years, but may be changed at any time. There can be several dens within the home range. Each consists of a nest of grass stuffed into a sheltered cavity. Typical locations include a hollow tree, a rocky crevice, a burrow, or even the corner of an attic or outhouse.

⊝ *Between leaving the pouch and achieving full independence, riding on the mother's back is the usual mode of transport for young Virginia opossums.*

## Hot-Tempered

Opossums are not territorial, but they are aggressive toward other individuals they meet. Males are especially hot-tempered; nonbreeding females less so. Rival opossums use threatening hisses and growls to warn each other off, building to harsh screeches through their 50 bared teeth. Fights are fairly common, but usually avoided by leaving regular scent marks around the home range. Such deposits provide clues to the movements of particular individuals, as well as information about their age, sex, status, and breeding condition.

Female opossums rarely live more than two years; and even if they survive into a third, they will not breed again. All their reproductive efforts must therefore be crammed into just two seasons. The breeding season is from January to August, giving most females the chance to rear two litters annually. Courtship is minimal, with every male approaching as many females as he can. In every month the female is only capable of conceiving on one or two days. If she is receptive, the pair will mate almost immediately. However, a male that approaches a nonestrous female will quickly be rejected.

Young opossums are born after just two weeks' gestation. Those that are lucky enough to reach the pouch spend a further 50 days firmly attached to a teat. Females usually have 13 teats (sometimes as many as 15). While most females give birth to about 20 babies, litters of over 50 are not unknown. Even in average-sized litters there are too many young for each to find a teat. The race to the pouch helps weed out the weakest individuals. It also ensures that the mother does not waste energy on young that are unlikely to survive. If only one or two babies reach the pouch, their feeble sucking is not enough to stimulate the production of milk. In such cases the litter is abandoned, and the whole process starts again.

Similarly, if a baby becomes detached from its teat before it can survive alone, the mother will ignore its cries, and it will die. This happens rarely, despite the inevitable crush in the pouch as the young grow and start to jostle one another. Once a young opossum starts to suck, the teat swells up inside its mouth so that it cannot let go. When the young are old enough to detach voluntarily from the teat, they accompany their mother out of the nest, riding in the pouch or on her back. They stay with her for a further month or two, becoming fully independent in just four months. Litters born in spring tend to disperse earlier than those arriving in late summer, which may stay with their mother throughout the following winter.

⊕ *A Virginia opossum feigns death to deter a potential aggressor. The condition, which brings on symptoms akin to fainting, can last for less than a minute or as long as six hours.*

## "Playing Possum"

**D**espite its reputation for aggression and belligerence, the Virginia opossum appears to know when it is beaten. Rather than try to fight an obviously superior rival or defend itself against a larger attacker, it resorts to the tactic of pretending to be dead. Various other animals employ a similar strategy, known as "playing possum." An opossum feigning death is amazingly convincing. The animal suddenly keels over on its side with its toes clenched, its body slightly curled, and its tail turned in as though it has died in the throes of some great stress or discomfort. At the same time, its mouth hangs open, and its eyes glaze over. The opossum does not flinch when handled and cannot be roused by loud noises or tickled, prodded, or shaken back to life. That deathlike state, called catatonia, can last for anything from one minute to six hours. Physiologically speaking, it is similar to fainting, but the opossum appears able to do it quite voluntarily. At the same time as "dropping dead," it allows a truly foul-smelling secretion to leak from its anus. The stench is usually enough to deter any other animal from inspecting the "corpse" too closely. The opossum waits for an opportune moment to "wake up" and make its escape.

*⊕ Virginia opossums do not hibernate and so need to forage all year round. Although they prefer to shelter in bad weather, they will sometimes venture out in snow and strong winds.*

## High Deathrate

Female opossums born in February may have litters of their own by August, but they are the lucky ones. The deathrate among opossums is high at almost every stage of their life. In the first few days failure to attach to a teat means starvation, and as many as 10 to 25 percent of young die in the pouch. Newly independent youngsters dispersing away from their mother are easy pickings for predators, and many starve or die of exposure during their first winter. Parasite infestations are common, as are other

## A Teaspoon of Babies

Newborn opossums are unbelievably tiny. Each one is smaller than a single pea and weighs about 0.007 ounces (one-fifth of a gram). Two hundred babies would weigh less than an ounce (28 g), and a litter of 20 can be carried in a teaspoon! Born after just 13 days inside their mother, they appear virtually embryonic. It seems unbelievable that such tiny, underdeveloped creatures can survive at all. Yet those 13 days have provided each baby with a heart, muscles and claws to enable it to crawl, and, somewhere in its minute brain, the will to face the immediate life-and-death challenge of reaching its mother's pouch and attaching to a teat. Doing so quickly is vital since there are rarely enough teats to go around, and babies that do not claim one will soon die.

diseases, although the species has a high level of resistance to rabies.

Roadkills account for thousands of opossum deaths every year; and as if that were not enough, many are trapped or poisoned as vermin or hunted for their fur. The fur industry peaked in the 1970s, when 1 million opossums were killed annually. Trade in opossum fur has since declined as a result of the relatively small profits to be made. At only $2 a pelt, hunting and skinning opossums is more effort than it is worth. Despite the many and varied perils facing the Virginia opossum, the animal's adaptable lifestyle and prodigious birthrate mean that the species continues to thrive.

⊖ *Infant Virginia opossums with their mother. In just 90 days they have gone from being smaller than a pea to the size shown here. But they are not safe yet. Newly independent youngsters are easy pickings for predators.*

## Conquering the United States

Before European settlers arrived in North and Central America, opossums lived only in the east—ranging from Nicaragua in the south to Pennsylvania in the north. While in Australia the arrival of colonists proved disastrous for its native marsupials, in the United States the Virginia opossum took readily to life alongside humans. By the late 1950s it had spread north to New York and the shores of the Great Lakes and west into the Great Plains states of Kansas, Nebraska, and Iowa. Much of the expansion was undertaken by the opossums themselves, as they exploited the agreeable living conditions around farms and gardens. The trend was sometimes assisted by deliberate introduction of the opossum to places such as California, New England, and Ontario (Canada). Today there are opossums all the way up the West Coast of the United States and Mexico (excluding Baja California). The range of the Virginia opossum is almost double what it was only 200 years ago, and it is still growing. Not bad for a "primitive" mammal!

# Australian Carnivorous Marsupials

Lots of marsupials eat meat as part of an omnivorous diet. However, the animals in this section feed almost entirely on other animals, from termites to spring lambs. The animals described in the following pages bear striking similarities to meat-eating placental mammals. Such similarities are a classic example of convergent evolution, in which comparable lifestyles lead to similarities in adaptations and physical appearance.

## What Are Carnivorous Marsupials?

There are three orders of carnivorous marsupial living in Australia and New Guinea, which until very recently contained six living families. The first and largest order, the Dasyuromorphia, contains the definitive marsupial carnivores—animals that feed almost exclusively on dead or live prey. There are three dasyuromorph families: the native cats and mice (Dasyuridae), the numbat, a marsupial anteater (Myrmecobiidae), and the thylacine, or Tasmanian wolf (Thylacinidae), which is now extinct. Most dasyuromorphs live in Australia, with a few in New Guinea and nearby islands.

The second largest order is the Peramelemorphia, containing two families of insect-eating bandicoots (Peramelidae and Peroryctidae). The third and most obscure group is the exclusively Australian order Notoryctemorphia, which contains just two species of marsupial mole in the family Notoryctidae.

Like placental carnivores, dasyurids have powerful jaws and sharp teeth. However, a smaller braincase and other differences in the shape of the skull mean that their faces are much more pointed. They can in fact look rather delicate, despite the presence of large, powerful jaw muscles. The teeth of dasyurids have sharp points for snagging, crushing, and tearing food. The canine teeth are large and pointed. In cross section they are oval—intermediate in shape between those of typical cats and dogs. The feet of dasyurids have five toes at the front and four or five at the back. The first digit of the hind foot (the hallux or big toe) is clawless, but all the other toes are armed with curved claws that are sometimes extremely sharp. Most dasyurids walk on the soles of their feet rather than the toes, and the underside of the whole foot is covered with tough, granulated skin.

The tails of dasyurids can be as different as the animals themselves. Tails can be long or short, fat or thin, and covered in sparse hair or dense fur. Some taper to a fine point; others end in an obvious tuft.

The majority of animals in this group are rather drab, with coats of uniform gray-brown fur, which may be

## Natural-Born Killers?

The carnivorous marsupials include some of the world's most rapacious predators. Members of this group often tackle prey larger than themselves, overpowering victims with sheer intensity of attack, and inflicting deadly crushing bites with sharp teeth. The largest living marsupial carnivore is the Tasmanian devil, a stout, doglike animal that can weigh up to 30 pounds (14 kg). Other much larger marsupial predators once dominated the food chain in Australia, but most died out in the last 5 million years. Despite its reputation as a savage and bloodthirsty killer, the Tasmanian devil is an intelligent and usually peaceful animal that scavenges much of its food from animals that are already dead. The smaller, less well-known members of the group are far more savage for their size. The world's smallest mammalian predators are marsupials—although which is the smallest is difficult to say. Adult ningauis or planigales often weigh less than 0.2 ounces (5 g). Both can kill and devour more than their own bodyweight in prey in a single night.

**SEE ALSO** Small Carnivores **1**:18; Large Carnivores **2**:8; Cat Family, The **2**:10; Dog Family, The **2**:50; Thylacine **10**:36

paler on the belly, but are otherwise generally unmarked. However, the larger members of the group include some of the most spectacularly patterned marsupials, with coats of glossy black and reddish brown and a variety of spots, stripes, and bands in differing shades from jet black to brilliant white. Seen clearly, the patterns appear very striking, but they all offer some degree of camouflage.

## A Group Apart

Many of the smaller marsupial carnivores lack a pouch. Some, such as the marsupial "mice" (antechinus), have small folds of skin on the abdomen that help protect young attached to the teats. Others, like the numbat, have long hairs on the belly that do the same job.

The bandicoots are an ancient group, separated from all other marsupials by millions of years of evolution. Like the other carnivorous marsupials, they have several pairs of front teeth (incisors) in the lower jaw, an arrangement known as "polyprotodonty." However, the bandicoots' feet are more like those of the great order of herbivorous marsupials, the Diprotodontia, having fused second and third toes on the hind feet. It is the combination of polyprotodont dentition and "syndactylous" digits that sets the bandicoots apart from all other marsupials. In terms of their lifestyle, however, they sit comfortably alongside the dasyurids because they feed mostly on live prey in the form of insects and their larvae. There are two families of bandicoot, both of which are adapted for digging, with strong front claws and a backward-facing pouch in the females.

# Dying to Breed

In several species the chances of a male living long enough to see his own offspring are very slim. In some species of phascogale, quoll, and most famously in the antechinuses or marsupial "mice," males invest so much in one massive breeding effort that a combination of stress, exhaustion, malnutrition, and immune failure kills them as soon as the breeding season is over. Females of the same species live longer and may breed more than once. However, second and third litters are usually smaller and weaker than the first.

⊕ *Some marsupial carnivores: kultarr (1); Pilbara ningaui eating a beetle (2); three-striped marsupial mouse (3); little red kaluta (4); fat-tailed pseudantechinus (5); narrow-striped dasyure (6); New Guinea quoll (7); red-tailed phascogale (8); short-furred dasyure (9); fat-tailed dunnart (10); common planigale eating a caterpillar (11).*

## Origins

The earliest marsupials in Australia were probably small insect-eaters that evolved to occupy a huge range of ecological niches. The bandicoots are thought to have split quite early from the other carnivorous marsupials and have changed little in 60 million years. The dasyurids, on the other hand, became very diverse. After 40 million years on Australian soil the group included a huge selection of marsupial predators. The cat, mouse, and mongooselike animals we know today are only the remnants of that once dominant group. Among the most impressive of extinct marsupial carnivores is a family of superficially wolflike animals called the Thylacinidae. The last member of the family was the thylacine, or Tasmanian wolf, which was driven to extinction by human persecution in the 1930s. At one time the Thylacinidae were thought to be close relatives of an extinct group of South American marsupials called the Borhyaenidae, but current opinion favors the theory that they were a late but rapidly evolving offshoot of the Australian dasyurids.

The third order of carnivorous marsupial has just one representative family, the enigmatic marsupial moles (Notoryctidae). Except for their deep, backward-facing pouch, they bear a strong resemblance to placental moles. Biochemical evidence, as well as feeding behavior, suggests they have a rather distant relationship to the other carnivorous marsupials. Moreover, they are the only Australian mammals to specialize in a burrowing lifestyle.

## Lifestyle

As a general rule, carnivorous marsupials are quick, agile animals that spend most of their lives at ground level. Some can climb quite well, but they lack the prehensile tail and specialized gripping feet of other more arboreal groups. They are generally active at night, although most species will emerge during daylight hours, and one, the numbat, only comes out during the day. The majority of species live solitary lives except when trying to breed.

↪ *The brush-tailed phascogale can descend a tree trunk headfirst, just as placental squirrels do. It can also erect the hairs on its tail, like a brush, which help assist balance when climbing.*

 **SEE ALSO** Devil, Tasmanian **10:28**; Dunnart, Common **10:38**; Mole, Marsupial **10:42**; Bandicoot, Northern Brown **10:46**

Since individuals rarely meet, scent and sound are important methods of communication because they can be effective over a distance and long time periods.

In many carnivorous marsupials, notably the bandicoots and some species of dunnart, reproduction is very rapid. Females produce large litters at a young age and raise them with minimum investment. Survival rates are low, but adults are soon free to breed again. Although there are reports of male Tasmanian devils providing food for females with babies, males are not normally involved in the rearing of young.

## Shrinking Habitats

Species of carnivorous marsupial are found in almost every conceivable habitat in Australia, from tropical rain forest to baking desert. However, the distributional ranges of the large species have undoubtedly shrunk in the years since European settlement. There are representatives of three families outside Australia, with several species of bandicoot, quoll, and marsupial mouse living in New Guinea and on surrounding islands. Many occur in forests threatened by human activities, such as timber extraction and slash-and-burn agriculture.

### Order Dasyuromorphia: 3 families, 18 genera, 64 species

**FAMILY DASYURIDAE (Australian carnivorous marsupials)**
16 genera, 62 species

*Dasyurus* 6 species, including northern quoll (*D. hallucatus*); New Guinea quoll (*D. albopunctatus*)

*Sarcophilus* 1 species, Tasmanian devil (*S. (laniarius) harrisii*)

*Antechinus* 10 species, including brown antechinus (*A. stuartii*); dusky antechinus (*A. swainsonii*)

*Dasycercus* 3 species, including mulgara (*D. cristicauda*)

*Murexia* 2 species, short-furred dasyure (*M. longicaudata*); broad-striped dasyure (*M. rothschildi*)

*Ningaui* 3 species, including Pilbara ningaui (*N. timealeyi*); southern ningaui (*N. yvonneae*)

*Parantechinus* 2 species, sandstone antechinus (*P. bilarni*); dibbler (*P. aplicalis*)

*Phascogale* 2 species, red-tailed phascogale (*P. calura*); brush-tailed phascogale (*P. tapoatafa*)

*Phascolosorex* 2 species, red-bellied dasyure (*P. doriae*); narrow-striped dasyure (*P. dorsalis*)

*Planigale* 5 species, including common planigale (*P. maculata*); Papuan planigale (*P. novaeguineae*)

*Pseudantechinus* 3 species, including fat-tailed pseudantechinus (*P. macdonnellensis*); Woolley's pseudantechinus (*P. woolleyae*)

*Sminthopsis* 19 species, including red-cheeked dunnart (*S. virginiae*); fat-tailed dunnart (*S. crassicaudata*)

*Antechinomys* 1 species, kultarr (*A. laniger*)

*Dasykaluta* 1 species, little red kaluta (*D. rosamondae*)

*Myoictis* 1 species, three-striped marsupial mouse (*M. melas*)

*Neophascogale* 1 species, long-clawed marsupial mouse (*N. lorentzi*)

**FAMILY MYRMECOBIIDAE (numbat)** 1 genus, 1 species (*Myrmecobius fasciatus*)

**FAMILY THYLACINIDAE (thylacine)** 1 genus, 1 species (*Thylacinus cynocephalus*)

### Order Peramelemorphia: 2 families, 8 genera, 21 species

**FAMILY PERAMELIDAE (bandicoots and bilbies)** 4 genera, 10 species

*Perameles* 4 species, including western barred bandicoot (*P. bougainville*); long-nosed bandicoot (*P. nasuta*)

*Isoodon* 3 species, including golden bandicoot (*I. auratus*); northern brown bandicoot (*I. macrourus*)

*Chaeropus* 1 species, pig-footed bandicoot (*C. ecaudatus*)

*Macrotis* 2 species; greater bilby (*M. lagotis*); lesser bilby (*M. leucura*)

**FAMILY PERORYCTIDAE (bandicoots and bilbies)** 4 genera, 11 species

*Peroryctes* 2 species, giant bandicoot (*P. broadbenti*); Raffray's bandicoot (*P. raffrayana*)

*Microperoryctes* 3 species, including mouse bandicoot (*M. murina*); striped bandicoot (*M. longicauda*)

*Echymipera* 5 species, including rufous spiny bandicoot (*E. rufescens*); Clara's echymipera (*E. clara*)

*Rhynchomeles* 1 species, Seram Island bandicoot (*R. prattorum*)

### Order Notoryctemorphia: 1 family, 1 genus, 2 species

**FAMILY NOTORYCTIDAE (marsupial mole)**

*Notoryctes* northern marsupial mole (*N. caurinus*); marsupial mole (*N. typhlops*)

**Common name** Tasmanian devil

**Scientific name** *Sarcophilus harrisii*

**Family** Dasyuridae

**Order** Dasyuromorphia

**Size** Length head/body: 21–31 in (53–80 cm); tail length: 9–12 in (23–30 cm); height at shoulder: up to 12 in (30 cm). Male bigger than female

**Weight** 9–26 lb (4–12 kg)

**Key features** Small, squat animal like a small bear; heavy-looking, muscular head; barrel body; short, furry tail; fur mostly dark-brown, lighter on muzzle; white chest band and patches on rump or flanks; female has 4 teats in a small, rear-opening pouch

**Habits** Nocturnal; usually solitary; aggressive to others of the same species

**Breeding** Two to 4 young born April–May after gestation period of 31 days. Offspring spend a further 105 days in pouch. Weaned at 8 months; sexually mature at 2 years. May live up to 8 years in captivity, 6 in the wild

**Voice** Growls, grunts, barks, and screeches

**Diet** Mostly wallabies, wombats, sheep, and rabbits taken mainly as carrion

**Habitat** Heaths, forests, and other well-vegetated areas

**Distribution** Australian state of Tasmania

**Status** Population: abundant. Protected by Australian law; extinct in mainland Australia, but widespread and abundant in Tasmania

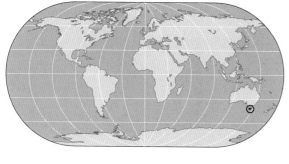

# Tasmanian Devil

*Sarcophilus harrisii*

*The Tasmanian devil's jet-black fur, fiery red ears, and huge, gaping jaws terrified early European settlers. Some believed they had encountered the "devil," but in fact the species is relatively docile.*

THERE IS NO MISTAKING THE Tasmanian devil for any other animal. Early European settlers in Tasmania (then called Van Diemen's Land) were horrified by the creature's blood-curdling screams and intimidating appearance. With its black fur, threatening toothy gape, and large ears that flush crimson or purple when the animal is excited, it seemed utterly demonic and soon became known as the "devil."

## Devil's Bounty

The scientific name *Sarcophilus* literally translated means "flesh-lover," a reference to the animal's ferocious appetite. Early encounters with large groups of snarling devils fighting over carcasses of wallabies, sheep, or cattle were largely responsible for the species' evil reputation. Devils were viewed as wanton killers of livestock and treated as vermin. The persecution reached a peak in the late 19th century. Every devil had a price on its head in the form of bounty offered by the Van Diemen's Land Company. The aim was quite simply to eradicate the entire species.

Ironically, the loss in the early 20th century of another persecuted carnivorous marsupial, the thylacine, probably helped save the Tasmanian devil. Faced with the reality of extinction, public opinion began to swing in favor of protection instead of persecution. Now that it is the largest surviving carnivorous marsupial, the Tasmanian devil is protected by law and has become the symbol of the Tasmanian National Parks and Wildlife Service.

Closer study of the Tasmanian devil has revealed it to be rather less sinister and

malicious than was once thought. Far from being wanton killers, the animals are in fact highly effective scavengers. They can kill birds, rabbits, snakes (including poisonous species), and young wombats with a bite to the head. However, even a large 22 pound (10 kg) devil would struggle to kill a healthy adult sheep. Devils certainly do not kill cattle, but they take full advantage of those that die from other causes. Before the disappearance of the

thylacine Tasmanian devils would have benefited from the remains of thylacine kills. Today a large part of their diet comes from animals killed by road traffic. Carrion is detected by smell and by the sounds of other devils feeding. The devil's massive head, powerful jaws, and fearsome-looking teeth enable it to crunch cartilage and bone so that nothing is wasted. Such an efficient disposal process actually provides a service to livestock

⊕ *The Tasmanian devil's ferocious appearance horrified early European settlers on the island. However, the animals are surprisingly timid when not competing with others for a share of scavenged carrion.*

farmers. Animal remains left to rot provide ideal places for blowflies to lay eggs and can lead to flystrike epidemics on farms. The devils prevent such an outbreak by eating dead animals before they become infested. Devils will also hunt smaller vertebrate and invertebrate prey.

### Feeding Frenzy

Tasmanian devils feed by taking the best of the flesh first, ripping it off in great chunks, and swallowing it almost without chewing. A devil can eat up to 40 percent of its own bodyweight of meat in a session. The way in which the animals bolt their food looks like greed. However, when several devils are feeding from the same carcass, it is the only way to ensure an equal share for each animal. In such circumstances there is always a lot of jostling for position, and the devils growl, scream, and bare their teeth at each other. Usually, however, they are too busy trying to get to the food to waste time in out-and-out fighting.

Although the scars carried by most adults are evidence that they do regularly bite each other, displays of bad temper are associated almost exclusively with food. Most of the time the devils live alone and are surprisingly timid creatures. The wide, yawning gape given by a cornered devil was once thought to be a display of threat and fury. It is now recognized as a sign that the animal is frightened. One scientist who handled over 7,000 wild devils claimed that, once captured, most were "docile to the point of lethargy."

### Population Boost

Devils today are found throughout Tasmania, sometimes in great abundance. In late summer numbers are especially high, since populations are boosted by the emergence of the season's young. Like the young of all marsupials, newborn baby devils are tiny and must complete their development inside the mother's pouch. The young—usually three or four at a time—are born in April (the fall). Each baby seeks out one of four teats in the pouch and remains firmly attached to it for about four

# Ousted by the Dingo

Tasmanian devils once lived all over Australia where—along with the thylacine—they would have been the dominant mammalian predators. However, all that changed with the arrival of the dingo from Asia about 4,000 years ago. The dingo is a far more efficient killer than the Tasmanian devil, and would have threatened it on two fronts: as a competitor for food and as a predator, especially of young devils. It is easy enough to imagine the devils being steadily driven back as the dingoes spread south. The theory is backed up by the fossil record, which shows that Tasmanian devils disappeared from the north of Australia about 3,000 years ago and from the far southeast about 600 years ago. The most recent devil remains, dating back to the 16th century, were found in Western Australia. The species was probably long gone by the time the first European settlers arrived in 1787. Since that time devils have been restricted to the island state of Tasmania, where they were protected from the advance of the dingo by the Bass Strait.

months. After this time it emerges into the den (a hollow log, cave, or old wombat burrow lined with leaves and grass) for short periods, returning to the pouch to suckle. The infants are weaned onto meat at five or six months old. Some reports suggest that the male devil may help care for some of his young at this time. However, adult males have also been known to kill and eat young devils.

At 10 months old the young devils are fully independent, and at this time the males in particular disperse to find a suitable home,

⊙ *The huge, yawning gape given by a cornered devil looks extremely ferocious. However, most devils are docile and unlikely to attack even when captured.*

generally moving about 6 to 19 miles (10 to 30 km) from their birth site. The deathrate is high among inexperienced animals. Hungry young devils that are unable to find enough food by night are sometimes seen during daylight hours. Once settled, an adult Tasmanian devil will occupy a home range of between 3 and 8 square miles (8 and 21 sq. km) depending on the availability of food.

Devils will travel 2 to 10 miles (3 to 16 km) a night in search of food. They generally move quite slowly, snuffling busily on the ground as they go. When speed is necessary, they use a bounding gallop. Most can climb, but the youngsters are more agile than the adults. Home ranges are by no means exclusive and can overlap with those of several other devils. In some parts of northern and eastern Tasmania the devil population sometimes exceeds 50 animals per square mile (20 per sq. km).

⊙ *Five Tasmanian devils squabble over meat from a roadkill carcass. Threatening behavior often occurs at joint feeding sites, but rarely progresses to real fights.*

# Northern Quoll

*Dasyurus hallucatus*

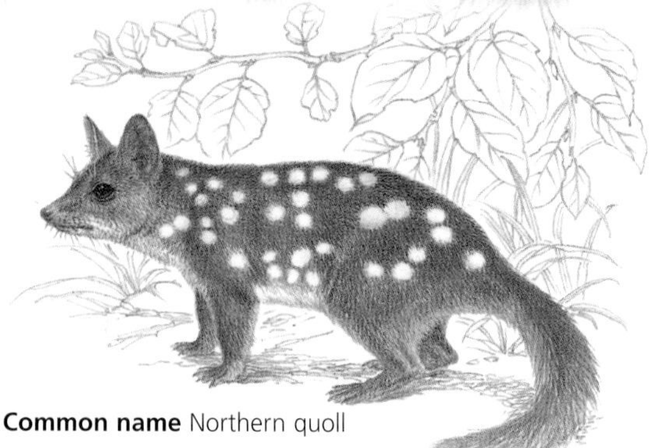

**Common name** Northern quoll

**Scientific name** *Dasyurus hallucatus*

**Family** Dasyuridae

**Order** Dasyuromorphia

**Size** Length head/body: 5–12 in (13–30 cm); tail length: 5–12 in (13–30 cm); height at shoulder: 4–6 in (11–15 cm). Male larger than female

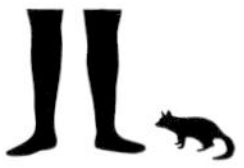

**Weight** 11–32 oz (300–900 g)

**Key features** Lithe-looking animal with long, thickly furred tail; small head with pointed snout; fur dark brown above, paler on underside; white spots on back; female has 6–8 teats covered by flap of skin when breeding

**Habits** Nocturnal; hunts in trees; solitary, territorial, and highly aggressive

**Breeding** One to 8 young born in July after gestation period of 21 days. Young remain attached to teats for up to 2 months. Weaned at 3–5 months; sexually mature at 10–11 months. Longevity unknown, but probably about 3 years in the wild

**Voice** Generally silent

**Diet** Small mammals, including rats; also reptiles, insects, worms, fruit, and honey

**Habitat** Wooded areas, usually within 90 miles (145 km) of the coast

**Distribution** Isolated populations in northern Australia, including parts of Western Australia, Northern Territories, and Queensland

**Status** Population: a few thousand; IUCN Lower Risk: near threatened. Has declined since European settlement; now protected

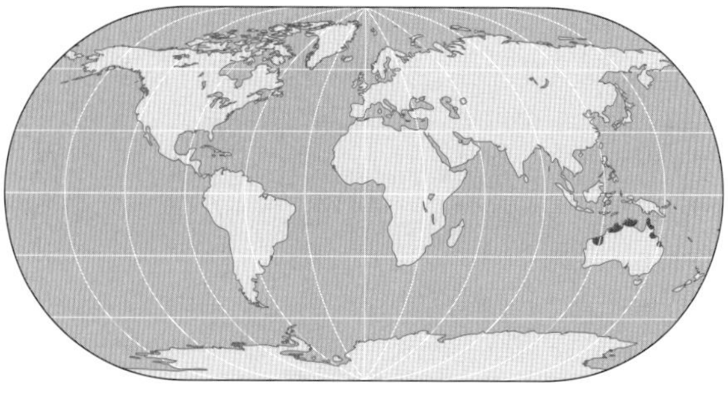

*The quoll is Australia's native marsupial equivalent of the cats that are widely found in the rest of the world.*

BEFORE HUMANS INTRODUCED predators like the dingo—and later the fox, cat, and dog to Australia—the only carnivorous mammals on the continent were marsupials. One group, the dasyurids, included a diverse range of predators that filled the niches occupied elsewhere by foxes, wolves, weasels, mongooses, and cats. Of the native Australian marsupial "cats," or quolls, the northern quoll is the smallest and reputedly the most aggressive.

## Catlike Hunters

Quolls are not particularly catlike in appearance. Their face is more pointed, and their tail is thicker and hairier. However, their hunting techniques are similar to those of small wildcats. The northern quoll specializes in hunting in the trees, but it is equally happy on the ground where it catches rats, lizards, and insects. Except for mothers with young, quolls live alone and will defend a core area of their home range against intruders. Within their territory the animals have several dens in hollow trees, rocky crevices, or sometimes abandoned buildings.

In some parts of its range the northern quoll lives close to human habitation. The species was once regarded as a potential pest and became rather rare as a result of persecution. Today it is legally protected, and most farmers regard it as a useful creature that is more likely to attack rats, mice, and insect pests than to kill poultry. Quolls also eat fruit and other vegetable matter, especially when water is in short supply. Where possible, they like to drink at least once a day.

Quolls have few enemies other than people. Their strong smell is off-putting to say the least, and few animals would want to eat them. Their extreme belligerence also makes

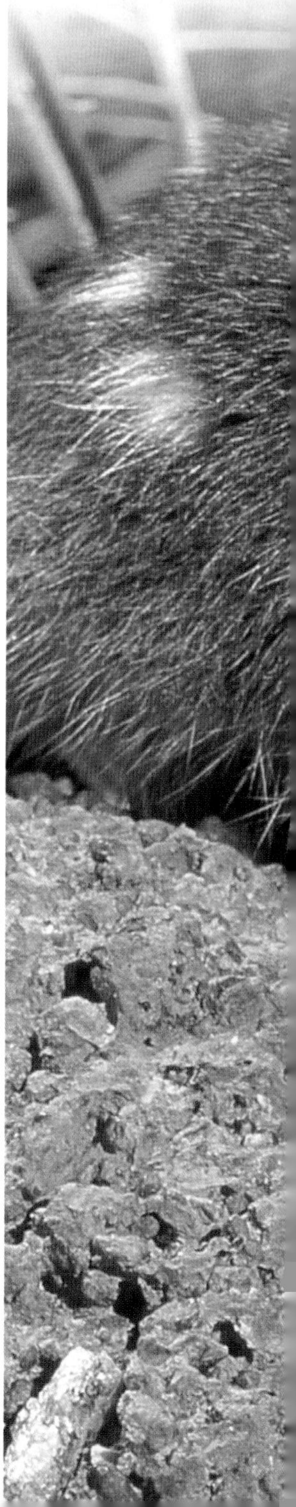

 **SEE ALSO** Weasel Family, The **1**:32; Wildcat **2**:48; Dingo **2**:80; Antechinus, Brown **10**:40

*While the northern quoll specializes in hunting in trees, it finds prey such as rats, lizards, and insects on the ground. It is the smallest and reputedly the most aggressive of the native Australian "cats."*

them a match for most predators. Quolls fight viciously when attacked or cornered, using their sharp claws and teeth to lethal effect.

## Burnout

Quolls have a similarly no-holds-barred approach to sex, and for a few short weeks in late June male northern quolls do little else. Being relatively short-lived animals with a single annual breeding season, male quolls have nothing to lose by putting everything into an all-out attempt to father as many offspring as possible. They hardly eat or sleep and often end up in serious fights. Courtship is also a rough affair, and the male often inflicts serious injuries on the female with his teeth. Shortly after mating, and even before the females give birth to their offspring, almost all the males in the population die of stress-related diseases. Those that survive are usually the less dominant individuals that mated relatively few females. But even they will die before the start of the next breeding season.

Female quolls lack a true pouch in which to carry their young. Instead, there is a simple fold of skin that partially covers the eight nipples. Most litters contain a maximum of eight young, each measuring just 0.12 inches (0.3 cm) at birth. Only the strongest six or seven will reach a nipple and survive to the next stage. The young quolls remain attached to the nipples for about two months. Any that drop off before that time face certain death. The youngsters then crawl onto their mother's back and begin taking solid food. Even when weaned, they still try to obtain milk from the mother, sometimes leaving wounds on her overstretched teats with their sharp little teeth.

**Common name** Numbat (banded anteater, marsupial anteater)

**Scientific name** *Myrmecobius fasciatus*

**Family**     Myrmecobiidae

**Order**      Dasyuromorphia

**Size**        Length head/body: 7–11 in (17–27 cm); tail length: 5–8 in (13–21 cm)

        **Weight** 11–23 oz (300–650 g)

**Key features** Vaguely squirrel-like animal with long, tapering tail and large feet with long claws; fur gray, tinged red on upper back, paler beneath; rump distinctly marked with white bars; muzzle long and pointed with small, black nose and erect ears; eyes large with dark stripe running through each; female has 4 teats, but no pouch

**Habits**    Solitary; active during the day; lively, nimble creature that climbs well

**Breeding**  Two to 4 young born December–April after gestation period of 14 days. Young carried attached to teats for 4 months. Weaned at 6 months; sexually mature from 9 months. May live at least 6 years in captivity, 6 in the wild

**Voice**     Soft snuffling sounds; hisses when disturbed

**Diet**        Mostly termites and ants; some other insects

**Habitat**   Dry, open woodlands and semidesert scrub

**Distribution** Southwestern parts of Western Australia

**Status**    Population: unknown, but declining; IUCN Vulnerable. Once found over much of southwestern and south-central Australia; now restricted to a few small areas in Western Australia; conservation has saved the species from extinction

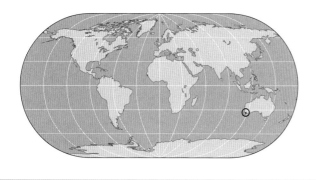

# Numbat   *Myrmecobius fasciatus*

*The numbat is the marsupial equivalent of the various types of anteaters that live in other parts of the world. Sadly, it has become a rare species, despite the abundance of food in Australia.*

THE NUMBAT IS A HIGHLY unusual mammal. It is different enough from all other marsupials to have been allocated its own family, the Myrmecobiidae. Most of the characteristics that set the numbat apart are associated in some way with its highly specialized diet.

## Termite Specialist

The numbat is the only marsupial that feeds exclusively on insects, predominantly termites. Termites are highly social insects that live in huge colonial nests in dead wood or soil. The numbat uses its strong claws to break open the nests. It probes the recesses with its long tongue, lapping up the insects as they scurry around trying to repair the damage. Often the numbat will also eat a few ants that happen to get in the way, but it does not actively appear to seek them out. More often than not the termites are swallowed whole, but some of the larger species may require chewing. For this the numbat has as many as 52 small teeth, more than any other land-dwelling mammal.

Termites are active during the day. As a result, the numbat is the only marsupial that is not even partly nocturnal. Numbats sleep all night, using burrows in winter and hollow logs in summer. These also provide valuable bolt-holes in which the numbat can escape from native predators such as eagles and other birds of prey. Today numbats also have to hide from introduced carnivores like foxes and cats. The new predators have taken a heavy toll on the numbat population. Before 1800 the species' distribution included much of southwestern

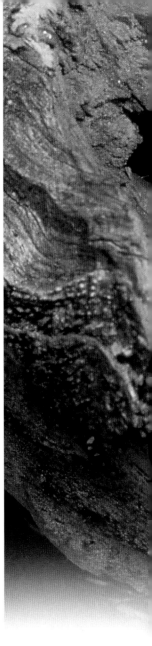

  **SEE ALSO** Fox, Red **2**:64; Fox, Bat-Eared **2**:76; Aardwolf **2**:110; Anteater, Giant **9**:68

*⊕ Hollow logs provide useful bolt-holes from predators, and also double as sleeping dens during the summer. Numbats sleep in burrows in the winter.*

Australia; but they were driven back by the invading predators, and numbers reached an all-time low of fewer than 1,000 animals in the 1970s. Numbats survived only in the south of Western Australia, where a species of eucalyptus tree, called the wandoo, provided places to hide from foxes and plenty of termite-infested logs. A series of fox-eradication programs has since allowed the recovery of numbat populations in some nature reserves.

Where the threat of predation is lifted, numbats can increase rapidly as a result of a relatively high birthrate and good parenting. Female numbats have four teats, and more often than not they will raise the maximum four young. However, there is no pouch, and for the first four months of life the babies must simply hang onto the teats to survive. They clamp their well-developed mouth muscles around the teat,

which swells to help increase their hold. The young are protected by a thick growth of fur on the mother's belly, but nevertheless their tenacity is amazing.

## Striking Out Alone

Toward the end of the suckling period the young are so big that their bodies drag along the ground as their mother walks. Once they detach from the teats, the youngsters spend a further two months in a secure nest. As they grow bigger, they emerge for longer and longer periods to play, bask in the sun, or learn the art of termite catching. They are fully independent by about nine months and will disperse over the summer to find a home of their own. Home ranges are large—up to 360 acres (150 ha). Numbats may behave territorially, excluding other adults of the same sex.

## Common name Thylacine (Tasmanian wolf, Tasmanian tiger)

**Scientific name** *Thylacinus cynocephalus*

| | |
|---|---|
| **Family** | Thylacinidae |
| **Order** | Dasyuromorphia |
| **Size** | Length head/body: 33–51 in (85–130 cm); tail length: 15–26 in (38–65 cm); height at shoulder: 14–24 in (35–60 cm) |
| | **Weight** 33–66 lb (15–30 kg) |
| **Key features** | Superficially doglike animal, with a long body and long, rather stiff tail; coat short and coarse; tawny brown with dark stripes across the back, rump, and base of tail; female has simple, crescent-shaped, rear-opening pouch |
| **Habits** | Active at night; usually solitary, although may have hunted cooperatively |
| **Breeding** | Two to 4 young born at any time of year (mostly in summer in Tasmania) after gestation period of about 1 month. Carried in pouch for 3 months. Weaned at about 9 months; sexual maturity unknown. (NB: all estimates from captive animals, situation in wild unknown). Lived up to 13 years in captivity, unknown in the wild |
| **Voice** | Whines, growls, barks, and sharp yaps |
| **Diet** | Mammals, including kangaroos, wallabies, smaller marsupials, and rodents; also birds |
| **Habitat** | Forests |
| **Distribution** | Widespread in Australia and New Guinea until about 3,000 years ago; restricted to Tasmania in historical times, but now extinct |
| **Status** | Population: 0; IUCN Extinct |

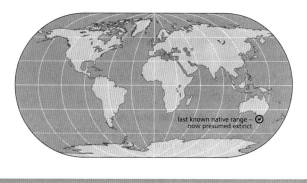

last known native range – now presumed extinct

# Thylacine

*Thylacinus cynocephalus*

*The thylacine is thought to have died out over half a century ago. However, occasional reported "sightings" keep alive the hope that a few might have survived.*

THE THYLACINE—ALSO KNOWN as the Tasmanian tiger because of its stripes and the Tasmanian wolf because of its doglike appearance—was once the dominant mammalian predator in Australia. It is one of the world's best examples of a phenomenon called convergent evolution, which occurs when animals with quite different ancestries evolve similar adaptations to help them exploit a similar ecological niche.

In Europe, Asia, and North America the niche for a large running predator that could catch and kill medium-sized herbivores was filled by wolves. Yet until recently there were no dogs of any kind in Australia. Instead, the thylacine evolved from the same stock as today's major group of carnivorous marsupials, the Dasyuridae. In South America another branch of marsupials called the Borhyaenidae gave rise to similar large predators, but they went extinct several million years ago.

## The Marsupial Wolf

While there are a number of striking similarities between the thylacine and a wolf, certain traits still mark the animal clearly as a marsupial. The most obvious characteristic was that females carried their young in a pouch. In addition, thylacine tracks showed five digits on the front feet, while those of dogs show only four toes.

The skeleton of the thylacine is similar to that of other carnivorous marsupials, with just a few proportional differences allowing the thylacine to run rather than leap or hop. Even so, by dog standards the thylacine was a relatively slow, awkward runner. It is thought that it relied more on stamina than speed to catch its prey, driving it at a swift trot until it was too exhausted to escape the large, snapping jaws full of sharp teeth.

**SEE ALSO** Wolf, Gray **2:**54; Dingo **2:**80; Quoll, Northern **10:**32

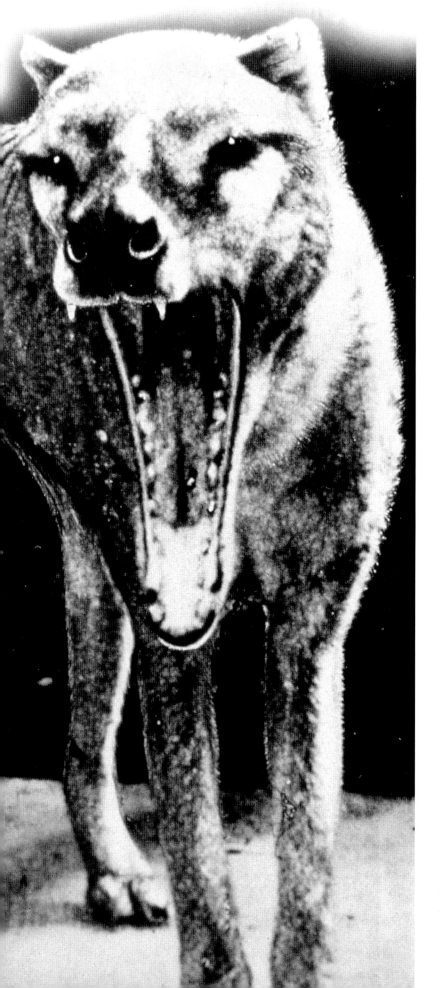

## Hounded Out

The tragic decline of the thylacine probably began between three and four thousand years ago when dingoes were first introduced to Australia from Asia: The dingoes were simply better at catching thylacine prey than thylacines. Being top predators, neither dingoes nor thylacines could live at high densities, and as a result, there was not enough room for both. The Tasmanian thylacine population was saved by the Bass Strait, which the dingoes could not cross, and the species continued to do well there until European settlers arrived in the 19th century. Used to wolf attacks on their livestock, farmers were quick to condemn the wolflike thylacine, yet there is little evidence to suggest they ever took a significant toll.

As early as 1830 the Van Diemen's Land Company (the governing body of Tasmania, formerly Van Diemen's Land) offered a bounty on thylacine scalps. By the mid-19th century thylacines were being shot, trapped, and poisoned without mercy. The government introduced its own bounty in 1888 and paid out on over 2,000 scalps before 1909. By 1920 the thylacine had all but disappeared, and its final decline may have been hastened by an outbreak of disease. In 1930 the last known thylacine was captured and taken to Hobart Zoo, where it died in 1936. The species did not receive legal protection until 1938.

Since then there have been numerous attempts to rediscover thylacines in the wild. Sightings are occasionally reported both on Tasmania and the Australian mainland; but none have been backed up with hard evidence, and most proved to be hoaxes or cases of mistaken identity. Nevertheless, large areas of Tasmanian wilderness have been designated as nature reserves in the hope that somewhere there may still be a small but viable thylacine population just waiting to be discovered.

⊖ *The last known thylacine, which died in Hobart Zoo in 1936. No specimens, alive or dead, have been found since, but claims of sightings are investigated seriously.*

**Common name** Common dunnart (narrow-footed marsupial mouse)

**Scientific name** *Sminthopsis murina*

**Family** Dasyuridae

**Order** Dasyuromorphia

**Size** Length head/body: 2.5–4 in (6.5–10.5 cm); tail length: 3–4 in (7–10 cm)

**Weight** 0.35–1 oz (10–28 g)

**Key features** Mouselike marsupial with long, tapering snout and long, thin tail; fur brownish-gray above, white below; female has 8–10 teats in pouch

**Habits** Active at night; hunts on the ground or leaps into the air to intercept prey such as moths; usually solitary

**Breeding** Litters of up to 8 young born August–March after gestation period of 13 days. Incubated in pouch for 40–45 days. Weaned at 65 days; females sexually mature at about 4 months, males at 5–6 months. May live up to 4 years in captivity, rarely more than 2 in the wild

**Voice** Squeaks associated with courtship and aggression

**Diet** Insects and their larvae, especially beetles; also spiders; will scavenge human refuse

**Habitat** Woodland and heathland

**Distribution** Southeastern Australia (Victoria, New South Wales, southeastern South Australia) and northeastern Queensland

**Status** Population: abundant. Common and widespread

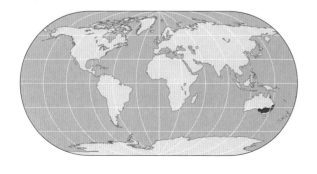

# Common Dunnart

*Sminthopsis murina*

*Dunnarts are small, mouselike carnivorous marsupials, also known somewhat clumsily as "narrow-footed marsupial mice."*

THERE ARE ABOUT 20 SPECIES OF dunnarts, 18 of which are found in Australia, (the other two occur in New Guinea). The common dunnart was once thought to range throughout most of southern Australia, but in the mid-1980s the "species" underwent a drastic reclassification.

## Scientific Advances

Reevaluation of the common dunnart was possible as a result of significant advances in biotechnology. New techniques allowed scientists to tell superficially similar animals apart by differences in their blood chemistry. When "common dunnarts" from different parts of the species' range were examined, it became apparent that there were in fact four species. They had previously been grouped together because they looked so similar.

Overnight the range of the common dunnart was roughly halved, but the animal still covers most of southeastern Australia and part of northeastern Queensland. Of the three new species, the little long-tailed dunnart (*S. dolichura*) and Gilbert's dunnart (*S. gilberti*) from Western Australia are fairly abundant. The newly named Kangaroo Island dunnart (*S. aitkeni*), on the other hand, gave much cause for concern. That was because only two individuals had ever been seen. Intensive searches have since yielded only six more of the Kangaroo Island dunnarts. Not surprisingly, there are fears that the newly recognized species may be on the verge of extinction.

The common dunnart is a nimble predator of insects and other small animals. It hunts by night and will snatch prey from off the ground or from the air, making huge leaps to intercept

*A male dunnart feeds on a cockroach. Insects make up a large part of its diet, and it is remarkably nimble in their pursuit, leaping up to swipe moths and flying beetles out of the air. It will also eat spiders and even scavenge human refuse.*

moths or beetles on the wing. When leaping or traveling at speed, the dunnart bounds along using only its hind legs, but mostly it moves on all fours. At certain times of year insects can be rather scarce, and during short periods of cold weather the dunnart may retreat to a nest and enter a deep, torpid sleep to save energy. Nests are used all year round as daytime hideaways, especially by females with young. They are particularly necessary for young that can leave the pouch but are not yet ready to venture into the world at large. The cup-shaped nest is made mainly of grass stuffed into a hollow log .

## Mating Call

Dunnarts are not generally territorial, but females with litters may be aggressive toward males. Individual males will also fight to establish dominance at the start of the breeding season. When they are ready to mate, females invite males to approach by calling. Births take place throughout the spring, summer, and fall, and there is time for three generations of females to breed in a good year.

Reproduction is potentially rapid, with a litter of up to eight young dunnarts being born and raised to maturity within four months. The first litter is able to breed while the mother is having a second and even a third litter.

## Boom and Bust

Several long-term studies show that common dunnart populations can fluctuate wildly from year to year. Such booms and crashes can often be linked to the burning of grassland and heathland. The fire is initially destructive, consuming the vegetation and almost anything else that might be eaten. However, the burning prompts the regrowth of young vegetation. Young growth exposed to the warm sun enables insects to flourish and provides plenty of food for dunnarts.

In the years following a burn dunnart populations boom, only to falter again when the plant community begins to mature. The trees and scrub develop, casting shade and reducing the quantities of insects at ground level.

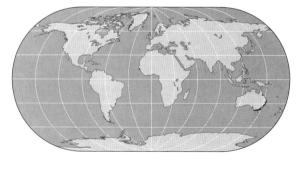

**Common name** Brown antechinus

**Scientific name** *Antechinus stuartii*

| | |
|---|---|
| **Family** | Dasyuridae |
| **Order** | Dasyuromorphia |
| **Size** | Length head/body: 3–5.5 in (7–14 cm); tail length: 2–4 in (6–11 cm) |
| | **Weight** 1–2.5 oz (28–70 g) |
| **Key features** | Mouselike animal with pointed nose, large ears, and long, hairy tail; coat is short, tawny to fawn, and paler underneath; feet are broad with 5 toes on each; first toe is small and lacks a claw; female has 6–10 teats, but no pouch |
| **Habits** | Active at night, usually terrestrial, but can climb well; males especially gregarious |
| **Breeding** | Six to 12 young born in October after gestation period of 27 days. Weaned at 3 months; sexually mature at 9 months. Females may live 2 years, males 11 months in the wild, not usually kept in captivity |
| **Voice** | Sharp squeaks given by males during aggressive encounters |
| **Diet** | Insects, especially beetles; also spiders, crustaceans, and other invertebrates |
| **Habitat** | Forest; also areas of scrub |
| **Distribution** | Eastern Australia: main population lives along coast of New South Wales and southern Queensland; second, smaller population farther north around Cairns |
| **Status** | Population: abundant. Common where it occurs |

# Brown Antechinus

*Antechinus stuartii*

*One of the marsupial "mice," the antechinus is actually more like a marsupial equivalent of the shrew. However, the species has an extraordinary sex life, which ends in an early death for the males.*

THE BROWN ANTECHINUS IS ONE of several dozen mouselike marsupials living in various parts of Australia and New Guinea. It mostly inhabits dense, wet forests, but will also colonize areas of scrub where there are plenty of good nesting places. For the most part it lives on the ground, but its wide feet with their ridged, "grippy" pads make it a proficient climber, and it readily takes to the trees.

The brown antechinus feeds on a variety of mainly insect prey. It is an efficient hunter, with adults managing to catch and eat about 60 percent of their bodyweight in beetles and other arthropods each night. In winter such food is less readily available. At this time of year the animals will also forage during daylight and may spend several hours a day in a kind of deep sleep, called a torpor. While sleeping, the brown antechinus saves energy so that it can survive on a reduced food intake. Sharing nests with a dozen or more other antechinuses also gives respite from the cold, and it seems that males never sleep alone.

## Life-Threatening Behavior

The breeding behavior of the brown antechinus is extraordinary. In spring males stop feeding and gather together in large numbers in special nesting trees. There will be a number of females in the trees, too, and others will visit from the surrounding area once the breeding season gets underway. The season is timed very precisely and is triggered by increasing daylight as spring approaches. In the runup to the season the males are highly aggressive, and a dominance hierarchy is established by fighting and threat

**SEE ALSO** Shrew Family, The **9**:28; Devil, Tasmanian **10**:28; Quoll, Northern **10**:32; Dunnart, Common **10**:38

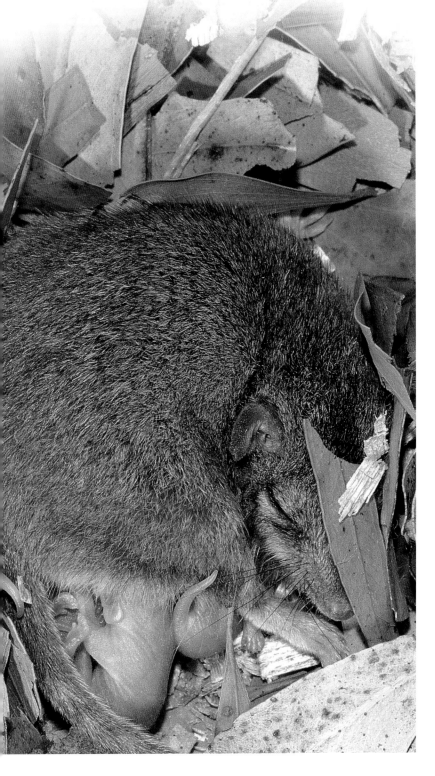

*⊕ A female antechinus suckles her young of six weeks. As with other species, such as the swamp antechinus, brown antechinus females have no pouch.*

males dash madly around in search of females, mate, and then move on to the next. There is no time to feed, and their bodies start to break down muscle, internal organs, and other tissues for fuel. The excessively high levels of testosterone and stress hormones in their blood disable their immune systems. Not surprisingly, they rapidly succumb to parasitic infections and other diseases, and by the end of the two weeks every single male is dead.

Meanwhile, each female goes on to give birth to about 10 minute babies, which she carries attached to her teats. She has no pouch, so the babies often get dragged along the ground as she moves around. After five weeks the young detach and remain in the nest, suckling occasionally for a few more weeks. They become independent at about three or four months old. Males only ever live for 11 months in the wild. Females can live longer, and some will breed in their second year, but such litters are generally very small.

## New Variety

Recently the brown antechinus of northern New South Wales and Queensland has been recognized as a different species from the antechinus of New South Wales and Victoria. The southern variety is now known as the agile antechinus. Much of what is written about the brown antechinus comes from studies of the agile antechinus. It may well be that when the Queensland species is studied in more detail, a few subtle changes will be made to the existing data on the brown antechinus. However, the fact that it has taken biochemical analysis to tell the two species apart demonstrates how similar they are, and it is unlikely that their behavior will be very different.

There are parts of New South Wales where both brown and agile species live side-by-side. However, there is no interbreeding because the two types mate at slightly different times of year. Breeding is so closely synchronized that it is impossible for a brown antechinus to mate out of season with an agile one.

displays. All the females come into season within two weeks of each other, and the dominant males mate with as many as possible.

Mating is vigorous and can last up to six hours. Consequently, the male's sperm has a good chance of fertilizing the female before she mates with another male. For two weeks the

**Common name**
Marsupial mole

**Scientific name** *Notoryctes typhlops*

**Family**    Notoryctidae

**Order**    Notoryctemorphia

**Size**    Length head/body: 4–6 in (10–16 cm); tail length: 1 in (2.5 cm)

**Weight** 1.2–2.5 oz (34–70 g)

**Key features** Flat-bodied animal with pale golden fur and very short legs; front feet spadelike; no functional eyes; ear holes hidden in fur; nose has tough shield; tail is short and stubby; female has 2 teats in rear-opening pouch

**Habits**    Solitary; "swims" through sand without creating permanent tunnels

**Breeding**    Details not known

**Voice**    Not known, but probably silent

**Diet**    Insect grubs and other soil invertebrates; captive individuals are known to eat small reptiles

**Habitat**    Desert

**Distribution** Central and northwestern Australia

**Status**    Population: unknown; IUCN Endangered. Feared to be in decline

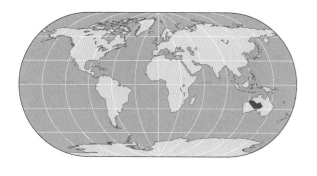

# Marsupial Mole

*Notoryctes typhlops*

*The marsupial mole is a strange creature. Although the marsupial equivalent of ordinary moles elsewhere, it is actually different from them in many respects. It is also sufficiently different from other marsupials to be classified in a group all on its own.*

THE MARSUPIAL MOLE IS PERHAPS the strangest of all marsupials. It does not appear to have any close relatives, and certainly no other Australian mammal has become quite so specialized in a burrowing lifestyle. It has a fat body covered in silky soft, golden fur, short legs, a leathery stub of a tail, and a tough, horny nose shield.

## Buried beneath the Desert

The marsupial mole spends much of its life buried in the desert. It "swims" below the surface of the sand with the use of two enlarged, shovel-like claws on each of its forelimbs. It does not create permanent tunnels: The sand collapses behind it, leaving only a faint, oval-shaped trail of looser material that can be seen in carefully collected soil core samples. It spends most of its time at a depth of 4 to 8 inches (10 to 20 cm), but occasionally digs down 5 feet (1.5 m) or more. Just about the only food available under the sand is plant roots and buried insect larvae, which can presumably be detected by smell and touch, since the mole has no eyes and virtually nonexistent ears. However, the moles do occasionally come to the surface, usually after rain. When they move over the sand, their bodies leave distinctive furrows with marks on either side where they have used their legs to haul themselves along. Captive individuals have been observed to eat above ground; but if such behavior were common, there would be more wild sightings. Their remains might be expected to turn up more often among the feces and prey debris left by predators, for example.

People occasionally find marsupial moles on the surface, but they are usually dead or quite ill. Even apparently healthy individuals have proved impossible to keep in captivity for more than a few weeks. Nevertheless, the discovery of a marsupial mole nearly always causes a bit of local excitement, and the animal usually ends up in a museum or a university. The specimen count has been increasing at the slow but steady rate of five to 15 animals every 10 years. Little is known about marsupial mole ecology in the wild, and even their breeding remains largely a mystery. It appears from their burrows that they are solitary most of the time, but they must be able to find each other somehow in order to mate. The females have a pouch that opens to the rear so that it does not get filled with sand. One or two dead marsupial moles with young in a pouch (a maximum of two, one for each teat) have been collected, but the duration of pouch life and the nature of the mother's relationship with her young can only be guessed at.

*⊕ Captive marsupial moles have been known to feed above ground, where they will eat small reptiles. Beneath the surface almost the only food available is insect grubs and plant roots.*

## Second Species

The marsupial mole was first described in the 19th century, but there are now thought to be two kinds of these bizarre animals. The second, the northern marsupial mole (*N. caurinus*), was discovered in 1920 on the northwestern coast of Western Australia. It is a bit smaller than the southern variety and has a differently shaped nose shield and tail. So few examples of this northern mole have been found that it remains virtually unstudied. It is uncertain whether it deserves species status in its own right.

It seems unlikely that marsupial moles have many natural enemies. However, there are fears that populations could be at risk from changes in land management. For example, the burning of vegetation to encourage the growth of grass for farm animals is especially damaging. Efficient introduced predators, such as foxes, are also a threat. There is evidence that foxes catch and eat marsupial moles. However, since no reliable population estimates exist, it is impossible to say how significant a risk they really pose. In the absence of hard evidence the marsupial mole is given full legal protection as a precautionary measure.

**Common name** Bilby
(greater bilby, rabbit-eared bandicoot)

**Scientific name** *Macrotis lagotis*

**Family** Peramelidae

**Order** Peramelemorphia

**Size** Length head/body: 12–14 in (30–55 cm); tail length: 8–11.5 in (20–29 cm)

**Weight** 1.8–5.5 lb (0.8–2.5 kg)

**Key features** Rabbit-sized animal with slender legs, long, furry tail, pointed nose, and huge rabbitlike ears; silky fur is gray above, white below; first half of tail is black, while rest is white to the tip; female has 8 teats in backward-opening pouch

**Habits** Active at night; terrestrial, lives in burrows; generally solitary, but not territorial

**Breeding** One to 2 young (occasionally 3) born at any time of year after gestation period of 14 days. Incubated in pouch for 80 days. Weaned at 95 days; females sexually mature at 5–7 months, males at 9–13 months. May live up to 7 years in captivity, fewer in the wild

**Voice** Virtually silent, except for snuffling noises; may huff when threatened

**Diet** Mostly insects and other invertebrates; also some small vertebrate animals and plant material

**Habitat** Dry woodland, scrub, and grassland

**Distribution** Central Australia

**Status** Population: maybe low thousands; IUCN Vulnerable; CITES I. Range and population have declined greatly in recent times

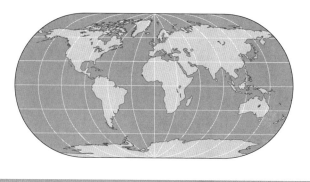

# Bilby

*Macrotis lagotis*

*The attractive long-eared bilby has suffered heavily from changes brought about by the European colonization of Australia.*

SINCE THE ARRIVAL OF EUROPEAN colonists in Australia about 200 years ago a host of desert animals have suffered declines due to hunting. They have also been decimated by introduced species of predators, such as foxes and cats, and faced severe competition with other nonnative species like the rabbit. Changes in their habitat brought about by new vegetation-burning projects or the introduction of grazing livestock have also had serious effects.

## Diminishing Range

The greater and lesser bilbies have suffered from all such threats. As a result, the lesser bilby is now extinct, and the remaining species is only found in a fraction of its original range. In 1800 there were bilbies throughout most of inland Australia. They had disappeared from New South Wales by 1912 and from South Australia by the 1970s. Today the only known populations are in the southeastern part of the Northern Territories and southwestern Queensland. Their range includes some of the driest, most hostile country in Australia. The poor red soils receive little rain and support only spiky spinifex grasses and scrubby acacias. A less hospitable spot would be difficult to find.

The bilby looks like an animal built of spare parts. Its rotund body is set on spindly legs that are longer at the back than the front. It has a delicate, pointed nose and vast pink ears. There is a long, furry tail, the second half of which is pure white, as though the artist decorating it ran out of paint. Surprisingly, these various parts fit together to rather charming effect, and the bilby is one of Australia's best-loved natives. Its habit of sleeping sitting up, with its nose tucked under its forepaws and its ears folded forward

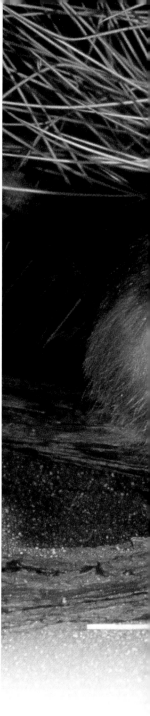

over its eyes serves to make the animal all the more endearing.

## Industrious Diggers

Bilbies are nocturnal and spend the daytime asleep in distinctive burrows. They are usually dug in the shelter of a grass tussock or termite mound. The burrows can be up to 10 feet (3 m) long and tend to spiral steeply downward to a depth of about 6.5 feet (2 m). Bilbies are such efficient diggers they can escape predators by extending the burrow faster than it can be opened up from the top end. They use the same industrious digging technique to find food. They excavate buried insect grubs that they detect by sound and smell, leaving dozens of 4-inch (10-cm) deep conical pits in the sand.

There is hardly ever any spare moisture in the central Australian desert, so bilbies must get all the water they need from their food.

In their current range bilbies breed all year round, only stopping if conditions get so harsh that litters would not survive. Females can breed more or less continuously. They ovulate and mate just before one litter finishes suckling, so that it can quickly be replaced with another. The young are nurtured in the pouch and then left in the nest to complete their development. Meanwhile, the mother goes out to feed, returning every so often to suckle her offspring. Male bilbies are usually solitary but may spend time with a female in order to mate with her. Males are aggressive to one another, but neither they nor the females defend territories.

⊕ *The greater bilby is seen here suckling its young. Habitat loss and predation have severely reduced its numbers, and the species is listed by the IUCN as Vulnerable.*

**Common name** Northern bandicoot (northern brown
bandicoot, large short-nosed bandicoot)

**Scientific name** *Isoodon macrourus*

**Family name** Peramelidae

**Order** Peramelemorphia

**Size** Length head/body: 12–18.5 in (30–47 cm);
tail length: 3–8 in (8–21 cm)

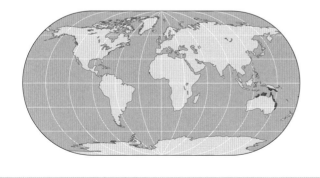

**Weight** 1.1–6.7 lb (0.5–3 kg)

**Key features** Rabbit-sized, ratlike animal with a long,
pointed face, glossy brown fur, long, hairy
tail, and very long claws; female has 8 teats
in rear-opening pouch

**Habits** Nocturnal; active on the ground; a solitary
and aggressive creature

**Breeding** One to 7 (usually 3 or 4) young born at any
time of year after gestation period of just
12.5 days. Incubated in pouch for 60 days.
Weaned at 8–10 weeks; sexually mature at 4
months. May live up to 4 years in the wild,
not usually kept in captivity

**Voice** Generally silent

**Diet** Insects, worms, and other invertebrates; also
some fruit, seeds, and nonleafy plant material

**Habitat** Open woodland and dense scrub, especially
close to rivers and swamps

**Distribution** Northern and eastern coasts of Australia,
New Guinea, and nearby islands

**Status** Population: abundant. Common within its
geographical range

# Northern Bandicoot

*Isoodon macrourus*

*The northern brown bandicoot is the largest, most
numerous, and most widespread of Australia's
bandicoots. It is also found in parts of New Guinea.*

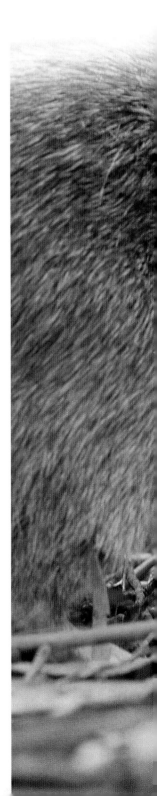

THE NAME BANDICOOT COMES from an Indian word
meaning "pig-rat," and at first glance the
animal looks like a large rodent. However, clues
to its true marsupial identity are easy to find.
Females have a well-developed rear-opening
pouch, which is almost always occupied due to
the species' prolific breeding habits.

## Double Toe

The bandicoot's feet are not at all ratlike: The
five toes of the front feet bear long claws, while
on the hind feet there appear to be just three
toes. Closer inspection reveals that there are
actually five. However, the first is small and
clawless, and the second and third are joined
together to form what looks like one toe with
two claws. The bandicoot uses its double toe
like a comb when grooming its fur. The
northern brown bandicoot has a long, pointed
face (although it is short-nosed in comparison
to other bandicoots, some of which have even
longer, narrower snouts).

The bandicoot favors dense, wet forests or
thickets with a good layer of undergrowth. In
the wet season the animal may emerge into
more open woodland or grassland to forage,
but the species' range is clearly limited by
average rainfall. Although bandicoots have a
varied diet, they mainly eat insects and their
larvae. They find food on the ground or just
below the surface by scratching with their
forefeet. Prey is caught under the front feet and
often pummeled to death before being eaten.

Northern brown bandicoots can also thrive
in parks, gardens, and other suburban habitats,
where their normal diet is supplemented by
food scavenged from picnic areas and garbage

⬇ *A female northern brown bandicoot forages on a woodland floor for insects and their larvae. Bandicoots find their prey by scratching on or just below the surface with their forefeet.*

cans. Such individuals become very bold and will even forage around the feet of humans.

Both male and female bandicoots are territorial and occupy well-defined home ranges. Both sexes build nests of twigs, leaves, and grass that they gather together in a heap over a shallow depression in the earth. The nest is often covered with a scattering of soil, which is added to when it rains in order to improve waterproofing. Bandicoots are antisocial and highly aggressive animals. Even mating pairs cannot stand each other's company for longer than is absolutely necessary. Males are especially bad-tempered and will fight for dominance using their claws and long canine teeth.

## Rapid Breeders

The northern brown bandicoot's main claim to fame involves its amazingly rapid rate of reproduction. It has the shortest gestation period of any mammal, with young bandicoots born just 12 days and eight hours after conception. Needless to say, northern bandicoot babies are incredibly small. However, once in the pouch, they develop quickly and can leave it after as little as seven weeks. The secret of their rapid progress is the mother's milk. It is thick and highly nutritious, containing over 40 percent solids (fat, carbohydrates, and proteins). There are usually about four young per litter, which leaves half of the mother's eight nipples unoccupied and ready to supply the next litter. The next batch of young is often born within hours of the pouch being vacated.

# Kangaroos and Wallabies

The kangaroos and wallabies are the most distinctive group of marsupials and also the most successful in terms of their distribution. They are well-known animals, owing to some types being very numerous and the fact that several species are large, conspicuous, and active in daylight. They have also been thoroughly studied because several of them compete with grazing livestock for food and are viewed as pests.

The group consists of 67 species of kangaroo, along with various wallabies, pademelons, potoroos, rat-kangaroos, and bettongs. With just one exception they all belong to one family, the Macropodidae. The odd one out is an animal called the musky rat-kangaroo, *Hypsiprymnodon moschatus*. A small, inconspicuous animal, it is classified separately on account of its unusual dentition and the fact that it has five toes on each hind foot. The musky rat-kangaroo is the sole survivor of the family Hypsiprymnodontidae, which represents an early evolutionary offshoot from the kangaroo family tree.

## Origins

In the early days of marsupial expansion in Australia, the land was covered in forests. Groups that had evolved a plant-eating way of life specialized in eating fruits, seeds, and sap, or browsed leaves from trees. The vegetation was luscious and fleshy, and much of it was relatively easy to digest. But as the continent of Australia drifted imperceptibly northward over millions of years, the

⊙ *A swamp wallaby browses on foliage. The species is the only member of the genus* Wallabia. *Despite its name, the swamp wallaby is found in upland forests as well as marshes and mangroves.*

## Order Diprotodontia (Part): 2 families, 16 genera, 67 species

**FAMILY MACROPODIDAE:** 3 subfamilies, 15 genera, 66 species

**Subfamily Sthenurinae (Sthenurines)** 1 genus, 1 species

*Lagostrophus* 1 species, banded hare wallaby (*L. fasciatus*)

**Subfamily Potorinae (bettongs and potoroos)** 4 genera, 9 species
*Bettongia* 4 species, burrowing bettong (*B. lesueur*)

*Potorous* 3 species, including long-nosed potoroo (*P. tridactylus*); long-footed potoroo (*P. longipes*)

*Caloprymnus* 1 species, desert rat-kangaroo (*C. campestris*)

*Aepyprymnus* 1 species, rufous rat-kangaroo (*A. rufescens*)

**Subfamily Macropodinae (kangaroos and wallabies)** 10 genera, 56 species
*Macropus* 14 species, including red kangaroo (*M. rufus*); eastern gray kangaroo (*M. giganteus*); red-necked wallaby (*M. rufogriseus*); common or hill wallaroo (*M. robustus*); whiptail or prettyface wallaby (*M. parryi*)

*Dendrolagus* 10 species, including Goodfellow's tree kangaroo (*D. goodfellowi*); Bennett's tree kangaroo (*D. bennettianus*)

*Petrogale* 13 species, including yellow-footed rock wallaby (*P. xanthopus*); Proserpine rock wallaby (*P. persephone*)

*Lagorchestes* 4 species, including spectacled hare wallaby (*L. conspicillatus*); rufous hare wallaby (*L. hirsutus*)

*Thylogale* 4 species, including red-necked pademelon (*T. thetis*); red-legged pademelon (*T. stigmatica*)

*Onychogalea* 3 species, including bridled nail-tailed wallaby (*O. fraenata*); northern nail-tailed wallaby (*O. unguifera*)

*Dorcopsis* 4 species, including white-striped dorcopsis (*D. hageni*); gray dorcopsis (*D. luctuosa*)

*Dorcopsulus* 2 species, Papuan forest wallaby (*D. macleayi*); lesser forest wallaby (*D. vanheurni*)

*Setonix* 1 species, quokka (*S. brachyurus*)

*Wallabia* 1 species, swamp wallaby (*W. bicolor*)

**FAMILY HYPSIPRYMNODONTIDAE:** 1 genus, 1 species

*Hypsiprymnodon* musky rat-kangaroo (*H. moschatus*)

**SEE ALSO** Kangaroo, Red **10**:54; Kangaroo, Gray **10**:60; Potoroo **10**:72; Marsupials, Other Plant-Eating **10**:74

climate began to change. Rains began to fall more infrequently, and consequently the forests dwindled and died. They were replaced by grassland, which was much tougher and more resistant to drought. For many forest marsupials the change was too drastic, and they died out. Others became even more specialized. They managed to survive in the reduced forests by being more efficient leaf, fruit, or sap feeders than their competitors. Some early kangaroos began to concentrate on roots and tubers, while others began eating grass.

But becoming grazers was by no means easy. Dry grasses are tough and in comparison with other plant foods contain little water, energy, or nutrients. It takes a highly specialized mammal to make a living from such

poor food. Kangaroos and wallabies—like other grazing mammals—depend on having lots of special symbiotic cellulose-digesting bacteria in their gut to help break down the tough plant material and release useful nutrients. The long intestine and partially compartmentalized stomach help slow the passage of food, allowing more time for digestion.

## What Is a Kangaroo?

Apart from the musky-rat kangaroo, all living kangaroos, wallabies, and potoroos belong in the family Macropodidae. As the name macropod ("big feet") implies, most members of the group have long hind feet. The fourth toe is greatly enlarged and along with the fifth bears the animal's weight. The second and third toes are small and joined together to form a kind of double toe, used for grooming. In all members of the Macropodidae (but not the Hypsiprymnodontidae) the first hind toe is absent. Compared with the hind feet, the front paws of macropods are relatively unspecialized.

The hind legs of kangaroos and wallabies are very large, with muscular thighs and long shins. The forelegs in most species are comparatively small, but the tail is

# Kangaroo or Wallaby?

The terms "kangaroo" and "wallaby" are not easy to separate scientifically. For practical purposes a wallaby is simply a small kangaroo. Large size is known to be an adaptation to life in open habitat. Therefore, a good rule of thumb is that wallabies tend to be found in less exposed terrain than kangaroos. However, to confuse matters further, in areas where there are no true kangaroos, people often refer to local wallaby species as kangaroos.

⬇ *Some examples of the larger species of kangaroo and wallaby: Proserpine rock wallaby (1); common or hill wallaroo with young in pouch (2); bridled nail-tailed wallaby (3). In the larger macropod species all four feet are only used when moving slowly—for instance, when the animal is grazing.*

⊙ *The rufous hare wallaby is one of only two remaining hare wallaby species. It is listed by the IUCN as Vulnerable and survives on only two islands off Western Australia.*

branches of trees. The most agile among the group are the rock wallabies, which have large hind feet with special nonslip soles covered in granular skin. Using their tail as a counterweight, they can bounce around over boulders and along cliff ledges with astonishing speed.

Kangaroos have long, thin necks and narrow heads. Their eyes are widely set, and their ears are large and mobile. They have fleshy, muscular lips, capable of plucking delicately at selected vegetation, and their teeth show various adaptations depending on diet. In kangaroos and wallabies, which eat mostly grass and leaves, the lower incisors do not meet the upper ones. Instead, they bite against a pad of tough skin in the upper jaw, gripping the food so that it can be sheared against the upper incisors. The front cheek teeth

long in all species. In the larger macropods the tail is thick and muscular and is used to help support the kangaroo's weight when it is moving slowly. In many smaller species it is carried off the ground and used to maintain balance.

Kangaroos are famous for hopping, which they do extremely efficiently at speeds of up to 35 miles per hour (55 km/h). However, all species can also get around on four legs. In the largest macropods all four feet are used when moving slowly—when grazing, for example. Smaller species, especially the potoroos or rat-kangaroos, are more nimble on all fours. In the tree kangaroos the forelegs are relatively large and strong and are used for gripping branches and hauling the animal up into the

⊝ *Some of the small and medium-sized kangaroos and wallabies: red-legged pademelon (1); whiptail or prettyface wallaby, hopping (2); burrowing bettong (3); banded hare wallaby (4); rufous rat-kangaroo (5). The smaller macropod species are more nimble on all fours than the larger members of the family.*

(premolars) of such species drop out as the animal matures. They leave space for the large grinding molars, which move forward throughout life to compensate for wear. Rat-kangaroos, however, eat foods like fruit, root vegetables, and fungi, which need to be broken into bite-size pieces before chewing. In these species the upper and lower incisors meet so that they can be used for chopping and gnawing; the premolars are permanent and help reduce wear on the molars, which do not move forward. All kangaroos have well-developed jaws. They are jointed to allow side-to-side movement, which makes chewing much more effective.

## Convergent Evolution

At first inspection kangaroos appear to have little in common with herbivores of similar size on different continents. After all, you are unlikely to see an antelope carrying its young in a pouch or cattle hopping on two legs. However, these seemingly different animals share a common way of life that has led to some startling similarities. Both kangaroos and hoofed grazing mammals have grinding teeth, a long gut, and a large stomach populated by vital cellulose-digesting bacteria. Both are also vulnerable to predators and adopt lifestyles that help minimize the risk. In forests the animals tend to live alone, while on open ground they are part of alert groups. The head of a kangaroo is strikingly deerlike, with wide-set eyes that give good all-round vision and mobile ears that can track sounds accurately. Both kangaroos and ungulates can move at high speed over open ground. They have long legs and reduced toes as adaptations to running or hopping. The kangaroo's hopping gait is not that dissimilar to the leaps and bounds made by some gazelles. Both have the effect of confusing a pursuer while putting as much distance as possible between predator and potential prey. Yet kangaroos are marsupials, and ungulates are placental mammals. Each group has had a quite separate evolutionary history, but has developed similar adaptations to help cope with the same sort of lifestyle. The phenomenon is called convergent evolution—two groups of different animals sharing similar adaptations to the same way of life.

### Efficient Digestion

Kangaroos and their relatives owe much of their success to the efficiency with which they are able to exploit limited food resources in hostile environments, such as deserts, arid islands, and rocky outcrops. They can survive on poor-quality food by digesting it thoroughly. Nitrogen is the vital ingredient in all proteins. Kangaroos obtain nitrogen—even from the poorest fodder—with the use of their large, effective digestive system. The stomach is big, and when full, it can account for up to 15 percent of the animal's total body weight.

However, kangaroos do not necessarily eat a lot. In fact, weight for weight they eat less than other grazing animals like sheep. Desert kangaroos simply have highly efficient digestion. Some species even obtain extra nitrogen by recycling urea, a natural waste product excreted by most other animals.

Desert kangaroos and species living in other very dry habitats, such as the quokkas of Western Australia's offshore islands, are also extremely efficient when it comes to conserving supplies of water. They can go for weeks without drinking and obtain all the water they need from their food or by licking dew from leaves.

### Lifestyle

Most species of kangaroo are active mainly at night or during the twilight hours of dusk and dawn. However, most can also be seen during the day, especially the larger species living in more open habitats. Forest-dwelling macropods (including the smaller wallabies, tree kangaroos, and rat-kangaroos) are secretive and rarely seen either by day or night. Out in the open, kangaroos are more inclined to live in groups as a precaution against predators. However, even these associations (known as mobs) are rather casual compared with those of social animals like wolves, chimpanzees, or even deer. Mobs are dominated by large males. As they mature, males tend to disperse from the group into which they were born, but females remain. The females in a group are consequently more closely related to each other than the males.

Female kangaroos have a forward-opening pouch, within which they usually rear just one offspring (joey) at

a time. It takes between 150 and 320 days for a joey to emerge from the pouch. In some species newly emerged young are independent almost right away. In others, notably the large kangaroos, there is a long period of dependence on the mother for milk and guidance.

## Kangaroos and People

Most of the kangaroo family lives in Australia. However, a quarter of them (17 species) occur in New Guinea, including tree kangaroos and other forest specialists. Throughout their range, the relationship between kangaroos and people has been very mixed. The smaller species, many of which depend on forests, have suffered badly from land clearance.

The introduction to Australia of nonnative predators, especially dogs and foxes, has also had a detrimental

⊕ *A gray kangaroo mother and youngster keep cool by wallowing in a pool of water. Kangaroos mostly rest during the heat of the day, emerging in the evening to feed.*

effect on numbers of small macropods. In contrast, populations of several of the larger species appear to have boomed in the years since European settlement, benefiting from the creation of rich pasture land for grazing livestock. Kangaroos are so efficient at exploiting grazing land that they are regarded as pests in many parts of Australia and shot. Some species have also been hunted intensively for skins and fur—the toolache wallaby from South Australia and Victoria was hunted to extinction. Hunting is more strictly regulated now than in the past, but quotas remain high, and current harvests may be unsustainable.

**Common name** Red kangaroo

**Scientific name** *Macropus rufus*

| | |
|---|---|
| **Family** | Macropodidae |
| **Order** | Diprotodontia |

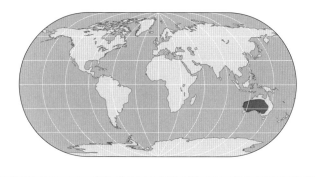

**Size** Length head/body: 29.5–63 in (75–160 cm); tail length: 25–47 in (64–120 cm); height: (upright) up to 6 ft (1.8 m)

**Weight** 37.5–198 lb (17–90 kg). Male may weigh up to twice as much as female

**Key features** Large kangaroo with rusty-red to blue-gray fur, paler on belly; female has 4 teats in a well-developed, forward-facing pouch

**Habits** Lives in loose groups; most active between dusk and dawn

**Breeding** Single young born at any time of year after gestation period of 33 days (plus up to 6 months delayed implantation). Incubated in pouch for 235 days. Weaned at 12 months; females sexually mature at 15–20 months, males at 20–24 months. May live more than 30 years in captivity, 27 in the wild

**Voice** Gruff coughing sounds

**Diet** Mainly grass; also leaves of other plants, including shrubs and trees

**Habitat** Scrub and open grassland, including arid and semiarid areas

**Distribution** Throughout central Australia; absent from the far north, eastern, and southeastern coasts, southwestern Australia, and Tasmania

**Status** Population: abundant. Remains common and widespread despite hunting and other control measures

# Red Kangaroo

*Macropus rufus*

*The red kangaroo is the tallest marsupial and the animal that comes to most people's minds when they think of Australian wildlife.*

THE RED KANGAROO IS THE archetypal Australian mammal, sharing pride of place with the emu on the country's coat of arms, and appearing in countless other emblems and advertising logos. The red kangaroo is the only large native herbivore to have conquered the heart of the world's driest continent and as such is of great ecological importance. Today it shares much of its range with sheep, cattle, goats, and even camels—animals whose impact has been greater because of the sudden nature of their spread, following introduction by humans. But the red kangaroo is a true desert specialist, and its lifestyle and physiology are better adapted to deal with the unforgiving, unpredictable desert climate than those of any imported mammal.

## Largest Marsupial

It is often said that the red kangaroo is the largest living marsupial, and in terms of height the statistic is probably true. But other large species, such as the wallaroo, can weigh more on average because of their stockier build. It is a close call. Male red kangaroos can stand over 6 feet (1.8 m) tall and weigh up to twice as much as the females. The disparity comes about because males compete physically for the right to mate and need to be large in order to succeed. Small males do not usually bother to challenge larger ones, so the genes for big, strapping males get passed on more often. Females do not need to be so big. For a start, they have to devote a good deal of their energy to rearing healthy young. In a hot climate the bigger you are, the harder it is to keep cool, so there is no advantage in large size unless you need to use it.

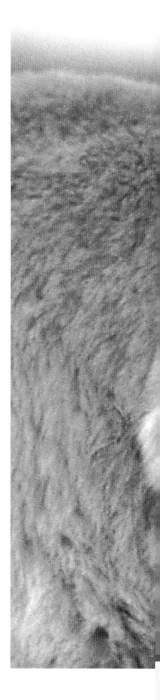

 **SEE ALSO** Camel, Dromedary **5**:94; Kangaroo, Gray **10**:60

Apart from its size the red kangaroo differs little from its close relatives in appearance. The red fur for which it is named generally occurs in males, while the females are a soft bluish-gray, hence their nickname "blue fliers." However, red females and gray males are quite common in some places, so color alone is not a reliable way of telling the sexes apart.

## Part Nomad

Red kangaroos are partially nomadic. While they will spend long periods in one area, if life should become difficult (as a result of environmental factors, such as drought or fire), or social causes (such as lack of mates or harassment from more dominant animals), they will undertake quite long journeys in search of better conditions. Individual animals have been tracked over 180 miles (290 km) before settling in a new area. Ideal red kangaroo habitat is an open grassy plain close to areas of scrub or open woodland, with a water hole nearby. Other requirements include shade from the midday sun and shelter from drying winds, but red kangaroos can make do with much less. Given a choice of fodder, they will eat mostly grass, supplemented with green leaves of other plants. They select the youngest leaves possible, since they are easier to digest. Every mouthful is chewed thoroughly so that the precious contents of plant cells are released ready for digestion. Like cattle and other ruminants, kangaroos have a large stomach containing bacteria that aid digestion.

The spread of sheep and cattle farming into central Australia has done much to improve the quality of grazing habitat. Boreholes bring drinking water to the surface for farm animals, and the grazing livestock keep down the rank vegetation, encouraging the growth of fresh new shoots. However, ranchers

⊖ *A juvenile red kangaroo. Red kangaroos are desert-living specialists that can cope with the extreme dry conditions far better than most introduced mammals.*

have been none too keen for kangaroos to share the newly created pastures, fearing that competition for food will disadvantage their stock. Such concerns have prompted much research into the precise feeding habits of several species of kangaroo. It appears that in favorable seasons there is no cause for concern. Livestock and kangaroos can safely graze side by side because—although both eat grass—about half the diet of each consists of very different kinds of greenery. None of the available food contains much water, and sheep and cattle have to drink regularly in order to survive. Kangaroos, on the other hand, are so well adapted to a diet of dry food that they actually lose weight if fed exclusively on lush vegetation. The water in the leaves takes up so much space that the kangaroo's relatively small stomach fills up before they have taken in enough real food.

### Survival Specialists

The potential for problems between kangaroos and livestock begins during prolonged drought. At such times the leafy herbs are the first plants to disappear, and both species turn their attention to the dwindling supply of withered grass. Ranchers try to fence kangaroos out of their pastures and shoot those that do get in. In severe droughts the survival of sheep and cattle depends on whether they receive supplements of food and water from the farmer. Meanwhile, the kangaroos usually survive, making do with the tough leaves of saltbush and other desert shrubs, whose high salt content makes them toxic to other animals.

Competition with livestock is not the only way in

which the interests of red kangaroos have conflicted with those of people. Many kangaroos are shot in an effort to prevent the damage they can do to rabbit fences. Rabbits are a far more serious threat to livestock than kangaroos, and special rabbit-proof fences are used to keep them out. But where kangaroos push down fences, they too are viewed as vermin and treated accordingly. Kangaroos are also hunted for their skins. Kangaroo hide makes fine leather, prized for making hats and soft sports shoes. Their meat, originally used in pet foods, is increasingly in demand as a tasty, low-fat alternative to beef.

Red kangaroos live in organized groups called mobs, usually consisting of one dominant adult male, with several females and young. Over a period of several weeks the members of

*⊕ Red kangaroos take time out for a drink. Since they are superbly adapted to living in dry conditions, they actually lose weight if fed exclusively on lush vegetation. In times of severe drought they get by through eating saltbush and other desert shrubs that are toxic to most mammals.*

## Boxing Kangaroos

**D**isputes between male kangaroos are usually solved by a display of size and strength, with the two contestants standing up on their straightened back legs. If one male is obviously shorter, he will usually concede and back off, but two closely matched males may escalate the encounter to a bout of boxing or wrestling. The opponents stand face-to-face, locking arms and trying to unbalance each other. In a full-blown fight they will leap into the air, swing their hind legs forward, and aim kicks at each other's chest and abdomen.

*Red kangaroos will often fight over access to females. Before a fight the two rival males may engage in a "stiff-legged walk." (1). They may also scratch and groom while standing upright on extended rear legs (2, 3). The animals then lock forearms (4), and try to push each other backward onto the ground (5).*

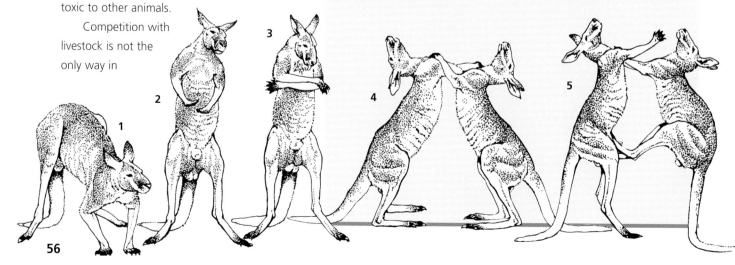

a mob may wander over an area between 600 and 1,200 acres (243 and 486 ha), but it is difficult to define a normal home range. Red kangaroos are certainly not territorial. The dominant male will do his best to ensure that he has exclusive access to the females in his group for mating purposes. The females, on the other hand, are pretty much free to come and go as they please. The male's control of the group is only ever temporary. The male may also defend good feeding areas from members of other mobs, but generally his aggression is reserved for rival males.

## Continuous Reproductive Cycle

Red kangaroos are opportunistic breeders, which means they can mate and give birth at any time of year, provided the conditions are favorable for raising a youngster. Females have a 35-day reproductive (estrous) cycle during which they will be receptive for less than a day. The cycle is not interrupted by pregnancy. It takes just 33 days for the baby kangaroo to develop inside its mother, so she is ready to mate again just a day or two after having given birth. Only when she is pregnant for the second time does the estrous cycle stop temporarily.

The change is triggered not by the embryo in her womb but by the newborn joey suckling on her teat. Having made its way to the pouch, the tiny morsel of a baby—the size of a jellybean and weighing less than a dime—attaches to one of four teats and stays there, growing steadily for 70 days. Meanwhile, the second embryo enters a period of suspended animation known as embryonic diapause. At this point it is no more than a ball of about 90 cells. It resumes its development precisely 33 days before the first baby (now 205 days old) is ready to leave the pouch permanently. Hence the second baby is born immediately after the pouch is vacant, and the female is ready to mate and conceive all over again.

The rather elaborate system means that a female red kangaroo can raise a baby every 240 days,

⊕ *Red kangaroos can mate at any time of year. The female will ideally have one offspring suckling, plus a second embryo in a state of suspended development, ready to be born once the first infant has vacated the pouch.*

like a factory production line, with no time wasted. More importantly, it means that if a joey should die or have to be abandoned due to a crisis (such as a fire that destroys all food or a drought), the second embryo can be immediately reactivated. The female then has another chance to raise a youngster without the need to find a mate. If there is a prolonged period of drought during which the female loses several babies in a row, her reproductive cycle comes to a complete halt, and she will not become fertile again until conditions improve.

# Hop It! Kangaroo Locomotion

Kangaroos are famous for hopping. In fact, they use two very different kinds of gait depending on how fast they wish to travel. For slow movements—when grazing, for example—they use all four limbs and the tail, and progress by means of a "five-legged" lope. The kangaroo leans forward and, with the weight of the body supported on its short front legs and the thick tail, swings both hind legs forward. It then lifts its front legs and tail and rocks forward until its weight is back on the hind legs. The tail is a vital part of this maneuver. It is strong enough to carry the animal's whole weight, and without it the front legs would be useless. For traveling at speed the front legs and tail do not touch the ground. The kangaroo leaps forward, using both hind legs to propel it anything up to 30 feet (9 m). The tail is used for balance. When pressed, a large kangaroo can easily hop at over 30 miles per hour (48 km/h). At one time it was thought that kangaroos might be unable to move their hind legs one at a time. In fact, the hind legs are perfectly capable of making independent stepping movements. However, they only do so when swimming. In water the kangaroo employs a cycling "dog paddle," much like any other four-legged animal.

→ *The red kangaroo uses its characteristic "hopping" motion to travel at speed. A large kangaroo can easily hop at over 30 miles per hour (48 km/h).*

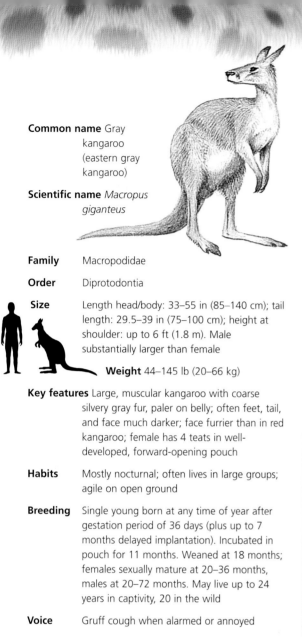

**Common name** Gray kangaroo (eastern gray kangaroo)

**Scientific name** *Macropus giganteus*

**Family** Macropodidae

**Order** Diprotodontia

**Size** Length head/body: 33–55 in (85–140 cm); tail length: 29.5–39 in (75–100 cm); height at shoulder: up to 6 ft (1.8 m). Male substantially larger than female

**Weight** 44–145 lb (20–66 kg)

**Key features** Large, muscular kangaroo with coarse silvery gray fur, paler on belly; often feet, tail, and face much darker; face furrier than in red kangaroo; female has 4 teats in well-developed, forward-opening pouch

**Habits** Mostly nocturnal; often lives in large groups; agile on open ground

**Breeding** Single young born at any time of year after gestation period of 36 days (plus up to 7 months delayed implantation). Incubated in pouch for 11 months. Weaned at 18 months; females sexually mature at 20–36 months, males at 20–72 months. May live up to 24 years in captivity, 20 in the wild

**Voice** Gruff cough when alarmed or annoyed

**Diet** Grass and other plant material

**Habitat** Scrub, woodland, and forest in areas with more than 10 in (250 mm) annual rainfall

**Distribution** Eastern Australia, including most of Queensland, New South Wales, and Victoria; also extreme southeastern part of South Australia and northeastern part of Tasmania

**Status** Population: abundant. Common and widespread; hunted under license

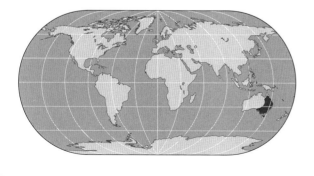

# Gray Kangaroo

*Macropus giganteus*

*The large gray kangaroo is extremely well adapted to life in open grasslands and has benefited from the extensive creation of grazing land for farm animals. It now competes with sheep for food and is even regarded as a pest.*

THE 18TH-CENTURY ENGLISH naturalist Thomas Pennant wrote about an animal that "...inhabits the western side of New Holland [the old name for Australia] and has yet been discovered in no other part of the world. It lurks among the grass; feeds on vegetables; goes entirely on its hind legs, making use of the forefeet only for digging, or bringing food to its mouth. The dung is like that of a deer. It is very timid; at the sight of man it flies from them by amazing leaps, springing over bushes 7 or 8 feet high and going progressively from rock to rock. It carries its tail quite at right angles with its body when in motion and when it alights it often looks back; it is much too swift for greyhounds; it is very good eating."

## "Giant Big-Foot"

So went Pennant's description for a kangaroo, which was given the scientific name *Macropus giganteus*, the "giant big-foot." However, it is difficult to know exactly which kangaroo he was referring to. The only large kangaroos on the western coast of Australia are wallaroos, red kangaroos, and western grays. The northeastern coast—from where the early expeditions of Captain Cook first brought detailed descriptions of these strange animals—is the home of the eastern gray kangaroo and the common wallaroo. Pennant's account could be applied equally well to any of these species. Indeed, in the early years of Australian natural history there appears to have been a good deal of confusion over which was which. Of three dead specimens that were originally used to describe

the species *M. giganteus*, at least one was apparently a wallaroo. The other two were eastern gray kangaroos. To begin with, it seems, the scientific name *Macropus giganteus* was liberally applied to any large kangaroolike animal. When it became obvious there was more than one species, zoologists had to decide which one got to keep the original name: In other words, which was discovered first? The problem was made all the more complicated by the fact that the early specimens had been lost or destroyed. Eventually, it was agreed that the eastern gray would from then on be *Macropus giganteus*, so becoming the first scientifically described kangaroo by default.

## Grazing Animal

The gray kangaroo is, like other large kangaroos, a grazing animal. It feeds mainly on grass and other low-growing vegetation, which it digests very efficiently. A gray kangaroo can survive on much less food than a sheep of the same weight. Even so, the gray is less well adapted to drought than the larger red kangaroo and so is only found in areas where there is a minimum of 10 inches (250 mm) of rain each year. That amount of

⊕ *The eastern gray kangaroo was first described by fascinated naturalists in the 18th century. Its scientific name means "giant big-foot." However, it appears that at least one of the first specimens recorded was in fact a common wallaroo.*

⇑ *A western gray kangaroo from Kangaroo Island, South Australia. The western gray is similar in appearance to the eastern gray kangaroo, and their ranges on the Australian mainland overlap considerably. However, the two species do not interbreed.*

rainfall is enough to support plenty of green vegetation, including trees, so the gray kangaroo usually has food and dense shade even when summer temperatures soar above 104°F (40°C). The adaptable species copes equally well with cold weather, and its range extends well into the southern temperate zone in Tasmania. The Tasmanian gray kangaroo is recognized as a separate subspecies, and not surprisingly one of its main distinguishing features is a thicker coat to keep out the cold.

## Mob Rule

Gray kangaroos are gregarious animals and tend to gather in large, loose groups called mobs, especially when feeding in the open. Individual kangaroos are not territorial, but within each group there is a hierarchy. Most groups are made up of adult females along with their offspring. Young gray kangaroos enjoy a prolonged relationship with their

mother, which often lasts long after they leave the pouch. Within a mob there are often several subgroups of two to five females and young animals, usually closely related.

The gray kangaroo is much more sedentary than its red cousin. Its apparent lack of wanderlust is largely due to the less fickle climate in which the gray kangaroo lives. There is usually plenty of green vegetation all year round, making large movements in search of food unnecessary. However, large adult males tend to wander between mobs, paying special attention to groups with females approaching estrus. The female is able to conceive once every 46 days. However, the big males will begin to show an interest days before the

## East Meets West

The western gray kangaroo, *Macropus fuliginosus*, was first described from Kangaroo Island off the coast of South Australia. It is in fact common throughout southern Australia, except in the extreme southeast. Its mainland range overlaps considerably with that of the eastern gray, and in large areas of New South Wales the two species live side by side. While they are very similar in size, appearance, and ecology, their breeding biology is so different that hybrids in the wild are unheard of. Western gray females have a shorter estrous cycle than eastern grays, and both gestation and pouch incubation times are shorter. Most importantly—in terms of keeping the two species separate—females of one species may refuse to mate with males of the wrong kind.

female is ready to mate. Males will fight for dominance and the right to breed, but a female has the final decision over which males she eventually mates with. Nevertheless, it is usually only the biggest and strongest males that are able to get anywhere near her when she is in breeding condition—the smaller males are forced to retreat.

## Embryonic Diapause

After mating, normal gestation takes just 36 days, and the baby gray kangaroo is born— blind, naked, and tiny. Unusually among the large kangaroos, gray mothers do not come into estrus again until the joey (offspring in the pouch) is at least four months old. She may

then mate once more, but the resulting embryo does not develop to more than a cluster of cells until its older sibling leaves the pouch at the age of about 11 months.

If the joey is lost (perhaps killed by a predator), the resting embryo can begin to develop immediately. The advantage of the arrangement is that the female does not have to spend time finding a new mate, and the rate of reproduction is not affected—compensating for young being born just one at a time.

The same phenomenon, known as embryonic diapause, occurs over a more extensive period in red kangaroos. Surprisingly, it does not occur at all in the closely related western gray kangaroo.

*⊕ Gray kangaroos live in loose groups known as mobs. Such groups are usually made up of adult females and their offspring; adult males will wander between mobs, trying to associate with females approaching estrus.*

**Common name** Red-necked wallaby (Bennett's wallaby)

**Scientific name** *Macropus rufogriseus*

| | |
|---|---|
| **Family** | Macropodidae |
| **Order** | Diprotodontia |
| **Size** | Length head/body: 26–35 in (66–89 cm); tail length: 24–34 in (62–87 cm); height at shoulder: about 30 in (75 cm). Male larger than female |

**Weight** 24–60 lb (11–27 kg)

| | |
|---|---|
| **Key features** | Medium-sized kangaroo with light-brown or grayish fur, reddish on nape of neck and shoulders; female has 4 teats in forward-opening pouch |
| **Habits** | Generally nocturnal; mostly lives alone or in small groups |
| **Breeding** | One (occasionally 2 or 3) young born at any time of year after gestation period of 30 days (plus up to 11 months delayed implantation). Leaves pouch after 280 days. Weaned at 1 year; females sexually mature at 14 months, males at 19 months. May live over 20 years in captivity, 18 in the wild |
| **Voice** | Occasional soft grunts |
| **Diet** | Grass and other plant material |
| **Habitat** | Various kinds of eucalyptus forest |
| **Distribution** | Southeastern Australia, including Tasmania; introduced to New Zealand and Britain |
| **Status** | Population: abundant. Common and numerous in most parts of its range; hunted for skins and as a pest in Tasmania |

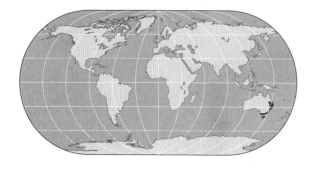

# Red-Necked Wallaby

*Macropus rufogriseus*

*Red-necked wallabies are typical kangaroos in many ways. But unlike most of their relatives, they have been successfully introduced outside Australia.*

RED-NECKED WALLABIES ORIGINATE from southeastern Australia. Here their range is restricted by a preference for densely vegetated eucalyptus forest in which to shelter.

## Separate Subspecies

There are two distinct subspecies of red-necked wallaby—one on the Australian mainland and the other on Tasmania. The Tasmanian subspecies is often known as Bennett's wallaby: It is bigger and heavier than the mainland variety and has thicker fur. Although not truly social animals, red-necked wallabies often gather in loose groups by a source of food or water. The composition of a group changes as individuals come and go at will, and there is little social interaction between unrelated animals. Young wallabies that have left the pouch and been weaned spend about a month hopping beside their mothers, after which their attentions are clearly unwelcome and they strike out on their own.

In mainland Australia there is no fixed breeding season, and mature females can come into estrus every 34 days all year round. The cycle continues when the female is pregnant, allowing her to mate within days of giving birth. It only stops when there is a youngster installed in the pouch and a second undeveloped embryo waiting inside the female. The second embryo resumes development when its older sibling leaves the pouch. As a result, mainland wallabies can raise one youngster every nine months. In the cooler, more temperate climate of Tasmania and on the islands of the Bass Strait breeding is more seasonal. Young red-necked wallabies spend winter in the pouch, emerging in summer when food is plentiful. The second embryo remains dormant much longer than in the mainland wallabies, eventually being born the following fall, about 11 months after conception.

The red-necked wallaby has adapted well to changes made in the Australian landscape by Europeans in the 200 years since colonization. Its distribution is little changed, and in some parts of its range—thanks to patchy forest clearance and the creation of grazing pasture— it is more common than before. The increase is especially apparent in Tasmania: The species thrives there despite strict measures to prevent wallaby damage to forests and plantations.

⊕ *Mother wallabies usually give birth to just one baby. However, the short interval between births means that they are often rearing an infant in the pouch while continuing to feed an older offspring that has reached the "young-at-foot" phase.*

Hunting for fur and skins is now only a small industry. The trade is centered on Tasmania, where red-necked wallabies are not only abundant, but have more valuable fur.

## Becoming a Nuisance

In 1879 several Tasmanian individuals were taken to Christchurch, New Zealand. From them a wild population developed in the nearby hills. But the introduced animals proved to be pests, damaging planted trees and competing with sheep for food. Over 100,000 were killed between 1947 and 1956. Even as late as the 1980s about 2,500 were shot each year. A small population also became established in the English Midlands, derived from escaped captive animals. But by 1999 numbers had dwindled to fewer than 20 animals. The newcomers are always elusive, but their tracks and droppings are quite distinctive. Sightings are occasionally reported by astounded walkers and motorists.

## Common name
Goodfellow's tree
kangaroo (tree kangaroo)

**Scientific name** *Dendrolagus goodfellowi*

**Family** Macropodidae

**Order** Diprotodontia

**Size** Length head/body: 22–30 in
(55–77 cm); tail length:
27.5–33 in (70–85 cm)

**Weight** 14–18 lb (6–8 kg)

**Key features** Small, slender kangaroo with legs of more
equal length than terrestrial species; fur is
woolly and reddish-brown, fading to yellow
on belly and feet; coat marked with 2 yellow
stripes down the back and pale rings on tail

**Habits** Arboreal; nocturnal; solitary, but not
antisocial

**Breeding** Single young born at any time of year after
gestation period of 21–38 days. Leaves pouch
after 8–10 months. Weaned at 13 months;
sexually mature at 2 years. May live up to 21
years in captivity, probably fewer in the wild

**Voice** Generally silent

**Diet** Leaves, flowers, grass, and fruit

**Habitat** Lowland and mountain rain forest up to
10,000 ft (3,000 m)

**Distribution** Eastern and central New Guinea

**Status** Population: possibly fewer than 1,000; IUCN
Endangered

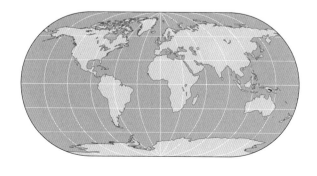

# Goodfellow's Tree Kangaroo

*Dendrolagus goodfellowi*

*While true kangaroos are adapted to life on the ground, tree kangaroos have conquered the arboreal zone up among the branches of trees.*

ONE OF THE FEW MEMBERS OF the kangaroo family to occur naturally outside Australia, Goodfellow's tree kangaroo is found across the Torres Strait on the island of New Guinea. There are 10 species of tree kangaroo, only two of which are Australian natives. Goodfellow's is one of the most attractive tree kangaroos, with rich, reddish-brown fur. Its belly, feet, and markings on its back and tail are pale yellow.

Unlike land-dwelling kangaroos, tree kangaroos have front and back legs of almost equal length. When on the ground, they move around with an ungainly rocking-horse gait, half hop, half jump. They cannot take long series of bounding hops because their tails are not strong enough to provide the necessary support and balance. However, their agility in the trees is more than adequate compensation for their relative clumsiness on the ground.

## Life in the Trees
The soles of the tree kangaroo's feet have rough pads ideal for gripping tree bark, and their claws are sharp and hooked. By spending a good deal of time off the ground, they can reach abundant food sources that other kangaroos cannot use. They are also relatively safe from most terrestrial predators, such as dogs. The tree kangaroo's favorite food is the leaves of the silkwood tree. It also eats leaves of other plants, including ferns. Other vegetable matter, such as fruit and flowers, is also eaten. Apart from a few insects accidentally swallowed along with other food, tree kangaroos have a relatively low-protein diet. They rely on an efficient digestive system to allow them to get maximum benefit from every mouthful.

⊕ *Goodfellow's tree kangaroo does not look or act much like the kangaroos and wallabies of Australia. It has traded the convenience of a hopping lifestyle for the security and food resources found in trees.*

The low-protein diet and the vagaries of New Guinea's tropical climate sometimes make conditions difficult for the kangaroos—especially nursing mothers. During periods of bad weather and food shortage the females become anestrous, meaning that they are unable to become pregnant. In some years there are hardly any young tree kangaroos (joeys) born at all. However, once conditions improve, breeding can begin again, and youngsters can be raised one after another every 10 or 11 months. Young tree kangaroos are born very small. Like other baby marsupials, they must make the perilous journey from the mother's cloaca to her pouch unaided. Once installed, they latch onto a teat and remain attached for between eight and 10 months. After that they climb out and begin to explore the world at large, but stay close to their mother for security. At this time they begin to eat leaves, but still return for a comforting drink of milk from the same teat they used throughout their development. The nutrient composition of the milk becomes richer as the joey develops. By the time the joey is almost weaned, there may well be a new baby in the pouch drawing a different kind of milk from another teat.

## Changing Fortunes

The landscape of New Guinea has changed dramatically over recent decades as a result of economic development. Mining and logging have led to habitat loss, and hunting for meat has also played a part in the tree kangaroos' decline. In places where the tree kangaroos live alongside agricultural land, they sometimes take to eating cereal crops. Despite their protected status, farmers are known to hunt them.

67

**Common name** Quokka

**Scientific name** *Setonix brachyurus*

**Family** Macropodidae

**Order** Diprotodontia

**Size** Length head/body: 19–24 in (48–60 cm); tail length: 10–14 in (25–35 cm)

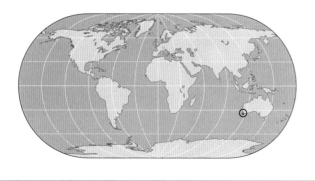

**Weight** 4.5–11 lb (2–5 kg)

**Key features** Small, grayish-brown furred wallaby with a short, sparsely furred tail; short, furry face with small, round ears; hind feet larger than front feet; female has 4 teats inside a well-developed, forward-facing pouch

**Habits** Nocturnal; normally ground dwelling, but can climb; often lives in groups

**Voice** Generally silent

**Breeding** Single young born at any time of year (seasonal in island populations) after gestation period of 27 days (plus up to 5 months delayed implantation). Leaves pouch at 6 months. Weaned at 9–10 months; females sexually mature at 8–9 months, males at about 14 months. May live at least 7 years in captivity, 10 in the wild

**Diet** Mostly leaves and shoots

**Habitat** Areas of dense, swampy vegetation in forests; also dry, open terrain

**Distribution** Localized populations in southwestern Australia; also on Rottnest and Bald Islands off Western Australia

**Status** Population: about 2,500; IUCN Vulnerable. Has undergone a serious decline

MARSUPIALS

# Quokka

*Setonix brachyurus*

*Quokkas are small wallabies and were one of the first of all the Australian marsupials to be discovered by European sailors.*

THE QUOKKA WAS ONE OF THE very first Australian mammals ever to be seen by European eyes. In the mid- to late 17th century Dutch ships exploring the west coast of Australia made various references to quokkas, but no one really knew what these unusual animals were. Marsupials were virtually unknown, and the quokkas were variously described as wild cats, civet cats, or most popularly, "rats the size of cats!" One of the islands on which the species still lives today was named Rat-nest (later Rottnest) Island because of the abundant quokkas that lived there.

## Primitive Characteristics

Quokkas are in fact a kind of wallaby. They differ from other members of the kangaroo family in several ways, mostly to do with blood chemistry, the structure of the skull, and the arrangement of their teeth—all of which appear rather primitive. Scientists generally agree that the ancestors of the quokkas split from the main branch of the kangaroo family tree quite early in the group's evolution. Quokkas were once widespread in southwestern Australia, but today they have a very restricted range. There are two populations on Rottnest Island and Bald Island, both off Western Australia, and a few colonies in specially conserved areas near Perth.

On the mainland quokkas live in dense, swampy vegetation where there is plenty of water and effective shade from the strong summer sun. In these relatively benign conditions the females breed at any time of year. However, the adults and young alike are at risk from introduced predators. For the island quokkas life could hardly be more different. The quokka population on Rottnest Island is one of the best-studied groups of marsupials in the

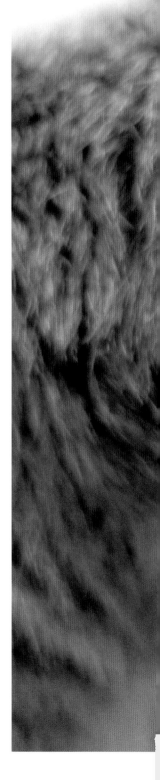

**SEE ALSO** Civet, Common Palm **1**:94; Wildcat **2**:48; Wallaby, Red-Necked **10**:64

world. Scientists are intrigued by how the animals have become adapted to the harsh environmental conditions, since their typical mainland habitat is much more supportive. Rottnest Island has climate and rainfall similar to the mainland—about 27 inches (690 mm) a year. However, unlike the mainland, any water that falls on Rottnest quickly drains away into the bedrock—there are no rivers. Since almost all the region's rain falls in the winter, summers on the island are both hot and extremely dry.

### Cold Sweat

The quokkas keep cool by sweating. They are able to survive for months on almost no water by switching their diet to more succulent plants. However, such plants are less nutritious than the quokkas' preferred food of dry herbage. By the end of the summer the animals are in a very poor condition, and there is often a large population decline. Under such circumstances the most critical resource on the island is neither food nor water, but shade. Shade is vastly important because animals that keep cool need to sweat less and so can afford to eat more dry but nutrient-rich food. Quokkas are gregarious animals, living in groups of 20 to 150, within which the males have a strict dominance hierarchy determining who gets the best shade.

Female island quokkas avoid rearing young through the summer, and so their breeding is much more seasonal than on the mainland. Both mainland and island quokkas can mate immediately after giving birth. They carry the second young as a dormant, or "diapausing," embryo while they rear the first baby. For the island females the second embryo is just an insurance policy: If the first offspring survives to weaning (by which time it will be almost summer), the second embryo is usually aborted. On the mainland it would resume development and be born soon after the pouch is vacated regardless of the time of year.

⊕ *Quokkas are a primitive type of marsupial only found in small pockets of southwestern Australia. The population that lives on Rottnest Island endures some of the harshest environmental conditions known to any mammal, since during the summer there is practically no water available.*

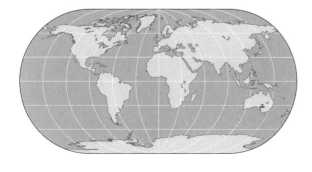

## Common name
Yellow-footed rock wallaby (ringtailed rock wallaby)

**Scientific name** *Petrogale xanthopus*

**Family** Macropodidae

**Order** Diprotodontia

**Size** Length head/body: 19–25.5 in (48–65 cm); tail length: 22–27.5 in (57–70 cm)

**Weight** 13–24 lb (6–11 kg)

**Key features** Small, gray kangaroo with orange-yellow ears, chest, legs, and feet; ringed tail; white underside; white cheek stripe; female has 4 teats in well-developed, forward-facing pouch

**Habits** Lives in small groups; mostly active at night

**Voice** Generally silent

**Breeding** Single young born at any time of year after gestation period of 31 days (plus up to 6 months delayed implantation). Spends further 194 days in pouch. Weaned at 1 year; sexually mature at about 18 months. May live up to 14 years in the wild, not usually kept in captivity

**Diet** Grass; also leaves of trees and shrubs

**Habitat** Rocky areas of semiarid plains

**Distribution** Flinders ranges of South Australia; also western New South Wales and south-central Queensland

**Status** Population: several thousand; IUCN Vulnerable; Declined in the past due to hunting; now strictly protected

# Yellow-Footed Rock Wallaby

*Petrogale xanthopus*

*Rock wallabies are small kangaroos that live among boulders and rocky outcrops, avoiding competition from their larger relatives out on the open grasslands.*

ROCK WALLABIES ARE AMONG the most attractive marsupials, with several species having richly colored fur and distinctive markings. The yellow-footed rock wallaby is perhaps the most decorative of them all, with its bright-yellow legs and feet, white cheek flashes, and a banded brown-and-yellow tail.

## Feet Made for Climbing

As their name suggests, rock wallabies are most at home in rocky country. Colonies tend to be centered on outcrops of rock with shady caves and crevices or boulder-strewn slopes with lots of long grass and other sheltering vegetation.

Rock wallabies are shy animals, preferring to keep out of sight as much as possible. They are able to move with astonishing speed and agility over the most awkward and treacherous-looking terrain. Their hind feet differ from those of plains-dwelling kangaroos: They are much better padded for protection against sharp, hard, and rough surfaces. Also, the claws of each middle hind toe, which in other kangaroos are large enough to provide traction, are short in the rock wallaby. Good grip is provided instead by rough, granular soles to the feet, which are fringed with stiff fur.

The yellow-footed rock wallaby's magnificent tail is long and furry, but not as thick at the base as that of a normal wallaby or kangaroo. It does not play quite the same role in supporting the body, but it is still important in maintaining balance on uneven ground. The rock wallaby carries its tail in an elegant upcurving arc when it hops from rock to rock, using it in much the same way as a tightrope walker uses a balancing pole.

Moving so skillfully over rocky ground takes a lot of practice as well as innate ability. Unlike young kangaroos, which follow their mothers on foot as soon as they leave the pouch, newly emerged rock wallabies spend their early days waiting in a safe corner while their mother goes off to feed. Trying to follow her is much too dangerous until they have learned the basics of negotiating rocks and unstable boulders. The young are also vulnerable to aerial attacks by wedge-tailed eagles, and each animal must be able to dart for safety at a moment's notice.

## Yellow-Footed Colonies

Yellow-footed rock wallabies are mostly nocturnal, emerging in daylight only during the winter when they bask in the morning and evening sun. Colonies of up to 100 animals occupy suitable areas of habitat within which the rocks can become polished and shiny from generations of furry feet. Individuals within a colony tend to stay in a home range of fewer than 500 acres (200 ha). Ranges overlap with many others, but interactions are generally peaceful. Breeding can happen at any time of year and regularly features a period of embryonic diapause. It allows a female with a youngster in the pouch to mate and conceive a second embryo. The second embryo remains dormant until the pouch is vacated.

Yellow-footed rock wallabies, along with several others of their kind, have suffered a marked decline in range and population in the last 200 years. The loss is due to excessive hunting for fur in the late 19th century and predation by introduced carnivores. The animals also face competition from other herbivores and pressure on their habitat from various kinds of land development. The species is now strictly protected throughout its known range.

⊕ *The yellow-footed rock wallaby is representative of the small- and medium-sized kangaroos and wallabies. Its feet are specially adapted to deal with the sharp, rocky terrain that characterizes its habitat.*

**Common name** Potoroo (long-nosed potoroo)

**Scientific name** *Potorous tridactylus*

| | |
|---|---|
| **Family** | Potoridae |
| **Order** | Diprotodontia |
| **Size** | Length head/body: 13–15 in (34–38 cm); tail length: 8–10 in (20–26 cm) |

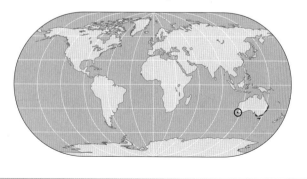

**Weight** 1.5–3.6 lb (0.6–1.6 kg)

**Key features** Compact, short-haired animal with thick, hairy tail; gray-brown fur, paler underneath; hind feet long with well-muscled legs; conical face with small nose, round ears, and large, black eyes; female has 4 teats in forward-opening pouch

**Habits** Shy; active at night; solitary; digs for food

**Breeding** Two litters per year, each of 1 young, born after gestation period of 4.5 months (including delayed implantation). Leaves pouch at 130 days. Weaned at about 5 months; sexually mature at 1 year. May live up to 12 years in captivity, 7 in the wild

**Voice** Generally silent

**Diet** Roots, underground shoots, tubers, fungi, insects, and other invertebrates

**Habitat** Coastal heaths and forest with dense ground cover in areas of high rainfall

**Distribution** Southeastern coasts of Australia, including Tasmania, Victoria, and New South Wales; also extreme southern corners of South Australia, Queensland, and Western Australia

**Status** Population: fewer than 10,000; IUCN Vulnerable. In decline since European settlement; now protected

# Potoroo

*Potorous tridactylus*

*Potoroos are small, ratlike hopping animals. They represent an early stage in the evolution of true kangaroos from more generalized marsupials.*

THE LONG-NOSED POTOROO belongs to a subfamily of marsupials commonly known as "rat-kangaroos." It has the distinction of being one of the first documented Australian mammals, having been noted by the first governor of Australia, Arthur Phillip, in 1789.

## The Missing Toe

A full scientific description followed a few years later, but the animal was mistakenly described as having only three toes on its hind feet (hence the scientific name *tridactylus*). In fact, as in most other kangaroos, there are four toes, two of which are joined to form one "syndactylous" digit. The musky rat-kangaroo (*Hypsiprymnodon moschatus*), a close cousin of the potoroo, has five hind toes. The family Potoridae is therefore thought to illustrate an intermediate evolutionary step between modern kangaroos and their five-toed ancestors. Potoroos are primitive in other ways: Their hind feet, while larger than the front ones, are nevertheless small compared with those of kangaroos. They can also still use their front legs for walking. Their tails are not as large as those of kangaroos and not as vital for balance and hopping. Instead, the tail is partially prehensile (able to grip), something wallabies and kangaroos have lost the ability to do.

The long-nosed potoroo is a variable species. Individuals from different parts of its range show marked differences in size and appearance. Queensland potoroos have a shorter nose than those in the south. In Tasmania most individuals have a white tail tip. Throughout their range potoroos are shy and difficult to see, only emerging a short distance from cover to feed at night. That partly explains why the Western Australian subspecies, known

as Gilbert's potoroo, was able to remain unseen for over 100 years from 1870, when it was first discovered. Indeed, the animal was thought to be extinct until some turned up in traps set to catch another small kangaroo, the quokka. The rediscovered Gilbert's potoroo is undoubtedly rare and in need of careful conservation if it is not to be lost a second time.

Potoroos forage by digging for fungi, insects, and plant material using the long, sharp claws on their middle front toes. Since most of their food comes from underground, the animals are well adapted to withstand certain hardships, such as the wildfires that frequently erupt in many parts of Australia. The animals spend the night moving around their home range, following well-used tracks. Territorial disputes are most common between males.

Females can rear two offspring per year, born one at a time. The second offspring is conceived around the time the first is born and remains dormant in the female's uterus until the older baby is weaned. The process—known as embryonic diapause—is common in marsupials.

## Cause for Concern

Potoroos everywhere have suffered a marked decrease in numbers. Their decline is partly due to natural climatic and vegetation changes, which over thousands of years have altered the major habitats of Australia. As a result, the potoroo's home has been pushed to the very edges of the continent. In the last 200 years the narrow strips of coastal forest have been disappearing even faster thanks to the expansion of human settlement and agriculture.

⊕ *A potoroo forages in the dense, damp ground cover of its forest habitat. It uses the long claws on its forefeet to dig up fungi, insects, and plant material.*

# Other Plant-Eating Marsupials

In addition to the kangaroos and wallabies there are another eight families of marsupials that specialize in a diet of plants. They include such familiar figures as the koala and common possum, as well as more obscure species, such as the agile pygmy glider and secretive spotted cuscus. Some of these herbivorous marsupials are among the world's rarest animals.

## Origins

The evolution of the plant-eating marsupials in many ways mirrors the development of mammalian herbivores on other continents. During the Cretaceous period (about 80 million years ago) most mammals were carnivores or insectivores, and the early marsupials were no different. However, during the later Miocene period flowering plants came to dominate the land. They created a new and abundant food source just waiting to be exploited by animals. Around the world specialized plant-eaters began to emerge, including primates, rodents, and hoofed animals. A similar evolutionary radiation happened among marsupial stock, giving rise to a group of animals with various adaptations to plant-eating lifestyles. As Australia's climate changed and previously forested areas were replaced with other habitats, several groups began to specialize in different types of plant. They developed new adaptations that allowed them to exploit eucalyptus

## Order Diprotodontia (Part): 8 families, 22 genera, 58 species

**FAMILY PHALANGERIDAE (cuscuses, brushtails, and true possums)**
6 genera, 20 species
*Phalanger* 10 species, including mountain cuscus (*P. carmelitae*); ground cuscus (*P. gymnotis*)

*Spilocuscus* 4 species, including admiralty cuscus (*S. kraemeri*); waigeou cuscus (*S. papuensis*)

*Strigocuscus* 2 species, small Sulawesi cuscus (*S. celebensis*); peleng cuscus (*S. pelengensis*)

*Ailurops* 1 species, bear cuscus (*A. ursinus*)

*Trichosurus* 2 species, common brushtail possum (*T. vulpecula*); mountain brushtail possum (*T. caninus*)

*Wyulda* 1 species, scaly-tailed possum (*W. squamicaudata*)

**FAMILY PSEUDOCHEIRIDAE (ringtails and other large possums)**
5 genera, 15 species
*Pseudocheirus* 8 species, including common ringtail possum (*P. peregrinus*); Daintree River ringtail possum (*P. cinereus*); Weyland ringtail possum (*P. caroli*)

*Petropseudes* 1 species, rock ringtail possum (*P. dahli*)

*Petauroides* 1 species, greater glider (*P. volans*)

*Hemibelideus* 1 species, brush-tipped ringtail possum (*H. lemuroides*)

*Pseudochirops* 4 species, including green ringtail possum (*P. archeri*); copper ringtail possum (*P. cupreus*)

**FAMILY PETAURIDAE (gliders and striped possums)** 3 genera, 11 species

*Petaurus* 6 species, including sugar glider (*P. breviceps*); mahogany glider (*P. gracilis*)

*Gymnobelideus* 1 species, Leadbeater's possum (*G. leadbeateri*)

*Dactylopsila* 4 species, including striped possum (*D. trivirgata*); Tate's triok (*D. tatei*)

**FAMILY BURRAMYIDAE (pygmy possums)** 2 genera, 5 species
*Cercartetus* 4 species, including eastern pygmy possum (*C. nanus*); western pygmy possum (*C. concinnus*)

*Burramys* 1 species, mountain pygmy possum (*B. parvus*)

**FAMILY ACROBATIDAE (feathertail possums)** 2 genera, 2 species
*Acrobates* 1 species, feathertail or pygmy glider (*A. pygmaeus*)

*Distoechurus* 1 species, feathertail possum (*D. pennatus*)

**FAMILY TARSIPEDIDAE (honey possum)** 1 genus, 1 species
*Tarsipes* (*T. rostratus*)

**FAMILY PHASCOLARCTIDAE (koala)** 1 genus, 1 species
*Phascolorarctos* (*P. cinereus*)

**FAMILY VOMBATIDAE (wombats)** 2 genera, 3 species
*Vombatus* 1 species, common wombat (*V. ursinus*)

*Lasiorhinus* 2 species, northern hairy-nosed wombat (*L. krefftii*); southern hairy-nosed wombat (*L. latifrons*)

 **SEE ALSO** Ruminants **6**:8; Kangaroos and Wallabies **10**:48; Kangaroo, Red **10**:54; Cuscus, Spotted **10**:82

woodland, scrub, grassland, rocky plains, mountains, and even the most hostile deserts on the continent.

## What Are Herbivorous Marsupials?

Along with the kangaroos, the herbivorous marsupials in this section constitute all the living species of the order Diprotodontia. The word diprotodont means literally "two first teeth" and is used to describe the condition of having just one pair of incisor teeth in the lower jaw. A single pair of lower incisors is one of the main defining characteristics of herbivorous marsupials. Another is the union of the second and third toes on the hind foot, giving the appearance of one digit with two claws. The phenomenon is known as syndactyly. Diprotodonts range in size from minute pygmy possums that can sit comfortably in a soupspoon to the red kangaroo, which is taller than a person and at least as heavy.

The largest marsupial herbivore, apart from the big kangaroos dealt with in an earlier section, is the common wombat. A squat, but hefty animal, the common wombat weighs up to 86 pounds (40 kg). Along with the koala,

the three species of wombat make up a distinct group within the Diprotodontia. The suborder Vombatiformes is an ancient offshoot from the kangaroo and possumlike branch of the marsupial family tree. Aside from the fact that koalas live in trees and wombats live underground, the animals have much in common. The similarities are particularly pronounced in their physical and behavioral adaptations to an extremely low-energy lifestyle. Also, the females of all four species have a rear-opening pouch, which makes sense for the burrowing wombats, but seems decidedly inconvenient for the arboreal koala.

Compared with koalas and wombats, which have robust physiques and a laid-back lifestyle, possums are mostly small and lithe, and lead active lives. Not surprisingly for forest animals, they climb well. They are helped by a long, prehensile tail used to grip branches. The palms and soles are also naked, often with rough or ridged pads to improve grip. Apart from in the honey possum—which differs from all other members of the Diprotodontia in so many ways that it is placed in a family on its own—all the toes except the first toe on the hind foot have long, curved claws. The first toe (or big toe) is opposable, meaning that it can be used to grip objects by folding against the sole of the foot. The possums were once classified together as one large group called the Phalangeridae. That larger group has more recently been split into five smaller families.

⊕ *Representative species of possums: a striped possum on a branch (1); a Leadbeater's possum feeds on sap (2); a common ringtail possum eats an insect (3).*

## Possums and Cuscuses

The best known possum is the brushtail—a common, widespread, and conspicuous animal that occurs in a wide variety of habitats. The brushtail comes from the family Phalangeridae, which contains 19 other species of possum and cuscus. The phalangers now living in Australia are ancient creatures that share similarities with fossil remains dating back 20 million years. The cuscuses have evolved more recently. They are the product of a few thousand generations of private evolution in the island forests of New Guinea, which was cut off from Australia about 7 million years ago. Possums and cuscuses climb well, but their movements are slow compared with many of their smaller cousins. Most species are general leaf-eaters, but fruit and flowers may also be taken.

The four other families of possum include the remaining long-tailed, tree-dwelling marsupials of wooded habitats in Australia and New Guinea. These species feed on various leaves, nectar, and sapgum. The most successful is the sugar glider, a small, squirrel-like animal. The mountain pygmy possum has abandoned the trees in favor of a terrestrial life on the boulder slopes of southeastern Australia's high mountains. For part of the year it is almost entirely insectivorous, feeding on the millions of bogong moths that migrate there to breed.

# Gliding

**P**erhaps the ultimate adaptation to life in the trees is the development of a gliding membrane or "patagium" that enables an animal to cover long distances between trees without descending to the ground. Among the herbivorous marsupials, gliding has evolved in three separate families: the Petauridae, the Acrobatidae, and the Pseudocheiridae. In all gliding marsupials, as in flying squirrels, "flights" are huge leaps in which the patagium is opened like a parachute to slow the rate of descent and control direction. However, most glides end in a scarcely disguised crash landing, with all four feet absorbing the shock of impact. By traveling in such a way, gliding marsupials are able to make more efficient use of a large foraging area than their evolutionary predecessors.

*Sugar gliders can collect the tree sap on which they feed by gliding from tree to tree.*

## Social and Reproductive Habits

The social and reproductive patterns of the various possumlike marsupials are as diverse as the animals themselves. In most species animals of both sexes use several nests within a home range. Often the nests are in tree holes or hollow logs; sometimes they are self-built twiggy structures called "dreys." In most of the larger

⊖ *In the summer the mountain pygmy possum switches from an insect diet to a seed-based diet. When its source of food dwindles, it stops feeding altogether and spends up to seven months in hibernation.*

species adults live alone except when breeding. Often, the ranges of males are larger and overlap with those of several females. The smaller possums tend to be more sociable, although the organization of groups varies between species. Adults may live alone, in mated pairs, or in mixed or single-sex groups of related or unrelated individuals. In most species the largest, fittest males mate with most of the females and dominate their social group, either by defending the largest home range or retaining exclusive rights to a large harem of females. However, in Leadbeater's possum the females are dominant and defend their own territories. They will drive away other females, including their own adolescent daughters.

## Balancing the Energy Budget

While some of the animals in this group of marsupials are generalist herbivores, most show at least some food preferences. Many are actually quite specialized. Whatever an animal chooses to eat, it must ensure it finds enough to compensate for the energy used in foraging, as well as fulfilling its everyday nutritional requirements.

Koalas and wombats exist on a low-energy diet of leaves and grass. Such foods have little nutritional value, but they are at least available all year round. Both koalas and wombats spend much time resting. They breed and develop slowly and have a thick coat and compact body to minimize heat loss. They can therefore get by on a diet that would starve many smaller, more active mammals.

At the other end of the scale are the small possums. Their energy needs are greater because of their active lifestyles, relatively greater strength, and rapid rate of heat loss. They also breed more rapidly. They eat concentrated foods like seeds, nectar, and sap. But such foods are not as easy to come by, and away from the tropics they are seasonal. When food is in short supply, the animals have to find ways of reducing their energy needs. Species like the pygmy glider do so by huddling together for warmth or entering a deep, torpid sleep for hours or even weeks.

# Teetering on the Brink

The specialized lifestyles of many marsupial herbivores allow them to share habitats with other species without coming into direct competition for resources. However, the very same adaptations can also make them vulnerable to changes that modify or destroy their particular niche. Many species, particularly forest dwellers, are now very rare. They have unfortunately fallen foul of the changes wrought on the Australian and New Guinean landscape in the last 200 years. Habitat loss and overdevelopment are threatening animals such as the mahogany glider, the mountain pygmy possum, Tate's triok, and several species of ringtail and cuscus. But the story is not all doom and gloom, and there have already been some notable conservation success stories involving herbivorous marsupials. The koala, for example, suffered dreadfully from overhunting in the 19th and early 20th centuries. By the mid-1920s it was facing a real crisis. The koala's plight awakened such public sympathy that hunting was outlawed, and the species was able to recover. Now it is one of the world's best-loved animals, and its future looks secure. In places there are even too many for the habitat to support.

# Common Brushtail Possum

*Trichosurus vulpecula*

*The common brushtail possum is a highly successful Australian marsupial that has learned to live with humans and exploit the opportunities they provide. It has also been introduced to New Zealand, where it has spread rapidly and become extremely abundant.*

ONE OF AUSTRALIA'S BEST KNOWN mammals, the brushtail possum is a highly adaptable creature and the most widely distributed of any native Australian marsupial. It feeds on a huge range of different native trees and shrubs, some of which are highly poisonous to other animals. The brushtail possum is a common nighttime sight even in towns and cities, where it lives quite happily alongside humans. It has found that attics and outhouses make a fine substitute for homes in tree hollows and rock crevices. In addition, its diverse dietary preferences are well served by the trees and other plants in orchards, parks, and gardens. Also, by scavenging from human refuse, the animals may easily acquire additional food. Their natural adaptability enables brushtail possums to occupy wooded habitats in every state of Australia.

## Nighttime Routine

Typically, the brushtail possum wakes up before dark, but does not emerge from its den until about half an hour after sunset. Often the animal does not go immediately to feed. Instead, it spends much time grooming its fine fur, which easily becomes matted. There is so much potential food around that only about 15 percent of the night will be occupied by feeding activities. Nearly a third of the time away from the den may be spent inactive. The animal returns to its den just before dawn. Heavy rain may delay emergence for up to five hours and will also cause the animals to seek shelter before the end of the night. Possums are mainly arboreal, but spend about 10 to 15 percent of

---

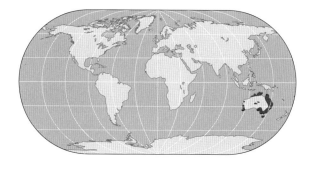

**Common name**
Common brushtail possum

**Scientific name**
*Trichosurus vulpecula*

**Family**    Phalangeridae

**Order**    Diprotodontia

**Size**    Length head/body: 14–22 in (35–55 cm); tail length: 10–16 in (25–40 cm). Male grows bigger than female

**Weight** 2.5–10 lb (1–4.5 kg)

**Key features** Large possum with oval ears and big brown eyes; fur grayish-brown in color; male often more reddish; long, furry tail is naked just under tip; large feet with 5 well-developed claws; second and third toes of hind feet are joined; female has 2 teats in well-developed, forward-opening pouch

**Habits** Active at night; largely arboreal; solitary; sometimes territorial; often found near human habitation and gardens

**Breeding** Single young (occasionally twins) born after gestation period of 17 days. Leaves pouch at 4 months. Weaned at 6 months; sexually mature at 9–12 months. May live up to 15 years in captivity, 13 in the wild

**Voice** Huffing, grunting, and clicking sounds; also loud screams when angry

**Diet** Mostly plants, including leaves, grass, seeds, flowers, and fruit; also invertebrates (such as insects); young birds and eggs; human refuse

**Habitat** Forests; cities and towns

**Distribution** Australia; introduced to New Zealand

**Status** Population: abundant. Common and widespread; considered a pest in New Zealand

---

⊕ *A common brushtail approximately six months old. If food is plentiful, it will stay with its mother for up to 18 months. If not, it will go its own way at about eight months.*

their time on the ground. Males generally have larger home ranges than females, but the ranges of both sexes often overlap, suggesting that the animals are not strongly territorial. In good lowland habitats there may be more than four possums per acre (10 per ha). While most young females settle in the area where they were born, three-quarters of young males disperse, sometimes traveling more than 20 miles (30 km) away.

Brushtails are agile climbers, capable of finding most of what they need to survive in the trees. However, they readily come down to the ground where it is necessary to do so. They have two opposable fingers (like thumbs) on each front foot and one on each of the hind feet to grip branches firmly. All but the first hind toes have sharp, sturdy claws. The tail is prehensile, with a hairless patch on the underside that helps improve its grip.

⊕ *Brushtail possums have two opposable fingers on each front foot and one on the hind foot. These allow them to grip branches firmly or manipulate food items.*

## Variations on a Theme

Not surprisingly for a species with such a huge natural range, brushtail possums from different parts of Australia show considerable variation in appearance and lifestyle. There are currently five recognized subspecies. One—the Arnhemland possum from the tropical northwest—was, until quite recently, thought to be a species in its own right. It has noticeably sparser fur, especially on the tail, the underside of which is often naked for much of its length. Other brushtails have a similar but smaller hairless patch under the tip of the tail.

Size variations are common among the other subspecies, with possums from Tasmania and Queensland being larger than those anywhere else. Color differences are also found. The Tasmanian subspecies, for example, is almost black, while the Queensland variety is mostly reddish brown. Possums from elsewhere tend to be a variable shade of gray, but males from all over Australia often have a swath of reddish fur around their shoulders. New Zealand fur traders recognize eight different color varieties within the species.

Population densities of brushtail possum vary with the quality of habitat. In turn, population sizes affect social behavior. Where food and nest sites are abundant, home ranges overlap considerably. Possums living in such rich habitats tend to avoid each other, but do not actively defend a territory. In poorer habitats, where the land supports fewer possums, the animals are less tolerant of each other. As a result, a more obvious social structure develops.

Scent and sound are used as territorial markers. Both males and females have anal, chin, and chest glands producing individually unique scents. The chest glands are particularly well developed in males, whose chest fur is often stained dirty brown by the secretions. Possum calls vary from gruff coughing sounds to rapid clicks, building to alarming screams in real anger. Frightened or angry possums make themselves appear as large and intimidating as possible by rearing up on their hind legs, raising their forelegs into the air, and screaming loudly.

## Outstaying Their Welcome— Possums in New Zealand

Brushtail possums were introduced to New Zealand in the mid- to late 19th century in order to create a fur trade. With no predators or real competition among New Zealand's native fauna the possum population boomed. Even intensive hunting did not seem to prevent the animals from thriving in their new home. In many parts of the country possums are still the most common animal seen dead on roads, even more so than rabbits. They live at higher densities in New Zealand than anywhere in their native homeland, with up to 20 animals occupying 2.5 acres (1 ha), compared with fewer than two in favorable parts of Australia. The possum fur industry remains lucrative in New Zealand, but nowadays the profits are offset by the considerable damage done by the animals, especially to agriculture. Possums destroy trees in plantations and orchards, and carry the bovine strain of tuberculosis, so posing a threat to cattle. Brushtail possums are now considered a major pest, but have so far survived all efforts to eradicate them from New Zealand's long list of troublesome introduced wildlife.

Such aggressive displays are usually enough to deter an intruder, but noisy fights are common.

Male possums are particularly aggressive during the breeding season, which in the north of the species' range lasts pretty much all year round. In the temperate south breeding is more seasonal. Female possums are polyestrous, which means they can breed more than once a year. However, they only do so if there is enough food to see them through pregnancy and a further six months of providing milk for their offspring. In the south of the possum's range most females breed just once a year—in the fall, although there is a second, smaller

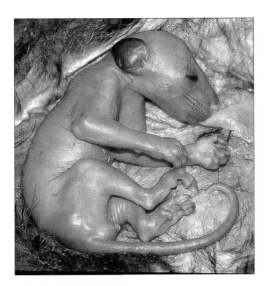

← *A young common brushtail possum attached to a teat in its mother's pouch.*

↙ *From four months the young possum will be carried around on its mother's back, returning to the pouch to be suckled.*

peak in the birthrate in the spring. Females in the tropical north may raise one litter right after another at any time of year, conceiving a new baby even before the last one is fully weaned.

Brushtails have two nipples, which restricts their litter size to just twins. However, while twins are sometimes known, single young are more common. The birth of triplets has occasionally been recorded in captivity, but in the wild the third newborn would certainly die. Young possums first emerge from the pouch at about four months old. They then spend a further two months riding on their mother's back, returning to the pouch to suckle. They learn to find adult food by sampling leaves from the trees in which their mother lives. They reach full independence at anything from eight to 18 months old, depending on the habitat. If food is plentiful, the mother possum will tolerate the presence of her older young for longer.

**Easy Prey**

The prolonged period of maternal care means that the infant death rate in brushtail possums is relatively low. Under favorable conditions populations can grow quickly, even without large litter sizes. The most dangerous time is the period between leaving the mother and settling in a new home. Young possums on the move are easy prey for dingoes, cats, and foxes, and many are killed on roads. Young animals are often forced to occupy poor-quality habitat.

**Common name** Spotted cuscus (common spotted cuscus)

**Scientific name** *Spilocuscus maculatus*

| | |
|---|---|
| **Family** | Phalangeridae |
| **Order** | Diprotodontia |
| **Size** | Length head/body: 14–23 in (35–58 cm); tail length: 12–17 in (30–43.5 cm) |

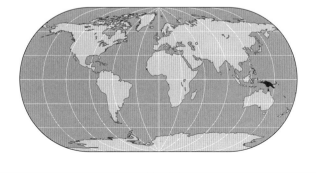

**Weight** 3.3–11 lb (1.5–5 kg)

**Key features** Large, long-tailed, woolly-looking possum with round head, small ears, and huge, round eyes; usually pale creamy-white with dark "saddle," often gray blotches (in males) or pale-gray body with pale patches in females; female has 4 teats in pouch

| | |
|---|---|
| **Habits** | Solitary; nocturnal; arboreal |
| **Breeding** | Little known. One to 3 young probably born at any time throughout the year. Gestation, weaning, and sexual maturity unknown. May live up to 11 years in captivity, unknown in the wild |
| **Voice** | Hisses, screeches, and clicks; females especially noisy when in breeding condition |
| **Diet** | Mostly fruit (such as figs), flowers, and leaves; probably also eats insects and other small animals it comes across |
| **Habitat** | Rain forest; also open woodland and mangroves |
| **Distribution** | New Guinea and surrounding islands; also Cape York area in northeastern Australia |
| **Status** | Population: abundant |

# Spotted Cuscus

*Spilocuscus maculatus*

*The spotted cuscus is the marsupial equivalent of sloths or slow-moving monkeys. It closely resembles them in appearance and habits.*

THE 15 KNOWN SPECIES OF CUSCUS were once all grouped together in the genus *Phalanger*. They originated on the island of New Guinea, from where some have made their way onto other islands and two have successfully colonized the northeastern tip of Australia. Recently it was agreed that the four species known as the spotted cuscuses differed sufficiently from the nonspotted species to be placed in a separate genus, called *Spilocuscus*. The genus includes three species that are confined to small areas of New Guinea and one, the spotted cuscus that remains relatively common and widespread and whose range includes Queensland, Australia.

## At Home in Trees

Spotted cuscuses are rather spooky-looking possums. Their round faces, huge, forward-staring eyes, and arboreal habits often cause them to be mistaken for monkeys. They are excellent climbers, but their movements are slow and deliberate compared with those of monkeys or other possums. They use all four feet and their prehensile tail to grip the branches. The tail is naked for much of its length and is covered on its underside with a number of little bumps or "papillae," which help improve grip. The rest of the body is covered in dense, woolly fur, which is generally creamy-white or gray in females. Males are white with large, gray spots.

Cuscuses are strictly nocturnal, but remain in the open by day, sleeping on branches in the canopy of rain forests. This sounds like a risky strategy, but in fact sleeping cuscuses are extremely difficult to spot. Before retiring at the end of each night, they build a loose platform of bent-over branches and leaves on which to lie down. The leafy bed effectively hides the cuscus from prying eyes below. During the night they move carefully around the branches, sometimes descending to the ground to cross open spaces to another tree nearby. They feed mostly on leaves and flowers, but the teeth of the spotted cuscus are still basically those of an omnivore, and meat may form part of the diet when it is available.

Scent is very important to spotted cuscuses. Glands in the face and under the base of the tail produce secretions that are spread onto branches and leaves. The facial gland is particularly active when the animal is stressed, leaking a reddish-brown substance onto the surrounding fur. A confrontation with an intruder, for example, might be enough to produce such a secretion.

Cuscuses leave trails of urine around their territory. They also dribble saliva on their hands and feet, spreading their personal scent to everything they touch. It may be that saliva evaporating from bare skin helps keep the cuscus cool in hot weather.

## Little-Known Breeding Habits

Little is known about the breeding biology of the secretive cuscus. The female has four teats in her pouch, but reports suggest that she is unlikely to rear more than one baby at a time. Like most marsupials, the male probably plays little part in rearing the young. Adult cuscuses are solitary animals, and males especially are known to fight fiercely by biting, boxing, and kicking in order to secure territory and access to females for mating. It is impossible to keep two males together in captivity. In the wild the less dominant individual would normally retreat and escape a serious mauling, but in a zoo enclosure or cage it has nowhere to go. The dominant male interprets the other's continued presence as a threat, and fighting will continue to the death.

⊖ *A white form of the spotted cuscus, mainly inhabiting rain forests and active at night. Like other varieties, its diet is made up of leaves, fruit, and flowers.*

**83**

# Pygmy Glider

*Acrobates pygmaeus*

**Common name**
Pygmy glider (feathertail glider)

**Scientific name** *Acrobates pygmaeus*

**Family** Acrobatidae

**Order** Diprotodontia

**Size** Length head/body: 2.5–3 in (6.5–8 cm); tail length: 2.7–3 in (7–8 cm)

**Weight** 0.4–0.5 oz (10–14 g)

**Key features** Tiny, mouselike animal with long tail, fringed with hairs on either side; feathery toes have round, expanded tips; fine web of skin stretches between front and back limbs on both sides of body; fur grayish above, white below; female has 4 teats in well-developed pouch

**Habits** Nocturnal; arboreal; glides from branch to branch

**Breeding** One to 4 young born after an unknown gestation period (including a variable period of delayed implantation). Births at any time of year in north of range, but during spring and summer in south. Leaves pouch at 60 days. Weaned at 95–100 days; females sexually mature at 8 months, males at 12–18 months. May live up to 7 years in captivity, about 3 in the wild

**Voice** High-pitched calls

**Diet** Insects and nectar

**Habitat** Dry forest and woodland

**Distribution** Eastern and southeastern Australia

**Status** Population: abundant. Common and widespread in suitable habitats throughout its geographical range

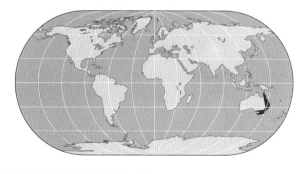

*The dainty pygmy glider is the world's smallest gliding mammal and one of Australia's most attractive and unusual wild creatures.*

THE PYGMY GLIDER'S TINY BODY is superbly adapted to life high in the forest canopy, where its feats of acrobatic skill are second to none. It is an agile climber, able to travel along even the finest branches. It keeps its balance by using its tail as a fifth limb. Smooth, hard surfaces present no obstacle, since the glider's toes bear large, finely ridged pads similar to those on a gekko's feet. If the surface is too soft, wet, or spongy for the pads to get a firm hold, no matter—the glider has claws sharp enough to do the job instead.

## Death-Defying Leaps

When the tiny pygmy glider reaches the end of a branch or wishes to move to another tree, it performs its best trick yet. It makes a death-defying leap into the air, spreading its legs and opening a web of skin—known as the patagium—along each side of its body. The gliding membrane allows the animal to proceed in a fast but controlled glide to a safe landing up to 70 feet (20 m) away. Other gliding mammals travel farther, but the pygmy glider is so small that the feat is equivalent to a human covering well over 1,000 feet (300 m) in a single leap. The speed and direction of the glide are fine-tuned with movements of the glider's unique tail. It is long and fringed on either side with straight hairs, hence the species' alternative name of feathertail glider.

Pygmy gliders are therefore able to make the most of the dense, three-dimensional habitat in which they live. They forage anywhere up to 130 feet (40 m) from the ground, seeking out insects and larvae from under tree bark and collecting blobs of

congealed sap from
branches or leaves. Pygmy gliders
also eat nectar taken from flowers.
Their teeth are sharp and numerous, as
would be expected of an insect-eater, but
their tongue has the brushy tip that is typical
of nectar-feeding animals. In cold weather,
when insect prey are hard to come by, the
gliders can spend a few days in a deep sleep
called torpor. During torpor their body
temperature drops as low as 35.6°F (2°C), and
their heart rate slows right down. Reducing
their activity and body temperature saves a lot
of energy. They can survive torpor for up to five
days, by which time—with luck—the cold snap
will have eased, and the glider can resume
normal activity.

Pygmy gliders build rounded nests by
stuffing leaves into hollow branches and other
crevices, including birdhouses. They are
remarkably nonaggressive animals, and a single
nest often contains several adults of both sexes.
Communal nests have been known to hold as
many as 20 individuals.

## Consecutive Families

Breeding occurs all year round in the tropics,
but is more seasonal in the temperate southern
part of the species' range. A female can rear up
to four young at a time (one for each teat in
her pouch) and can give birth to a second litter
as soon as the first is weaned. She achieves this
by mating right after giving birth, then keeping
the embryos of the second litter in a state of
suspended development until the first family is
almost ready to vacate her pouch. The young
are well cared for, and infant mortality is low.
After weaning some of the young remain with
their mother, which might help explain the
amicable sharing arrangements in some nests.

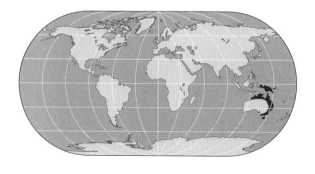

**Common name** Sugar glider

**Scientific name** *Petaurus breviceps*

| | |
|---|---|
| **Family** | Petauridae |
| **Order** | Diprotodontia |
| **Size** | Length head/body: 6–8 in (15–21 cm); tail length: 6.5–8 in (16.5–21 cm). Male larger than female |

**Weight** 2.8–4.8 oz (80–135 g)

**Key features** Small possum with long, furry tail and furry gliding membrane from wrist to ankle on either side of body; fur soft and pale gray with darker markings on face; dark stripe down back and on tail tip, paler on belly; female has 4 teats in well-developed pouch

**Habits** Social, but territorial; active at night; excellent climber and glider; bold and curious

**Breeding** Two young born June–July after gestation period of 16 days. Spend 70 days in pouch and a further 50 in communal nest. Weaned at about 3 months; sexually mature at 12 months. May live up to 9 years, usually fewer

**Voice** Grumbles, chatters, shrieks, screams, and high-pitched yapping sounds, mostly when angry, frightened, or disturbed

**Diet** Varied; includes plant sap and gum, pollen, nectar, fruit, honey, and seeds; also insects, spiders, and other invertebrates

**Habitat** Varied; anywhere with suitable food and nesting sites such as hollow trees or nest boxes; especially forests and wooded areas; tolerant of disturbance

**Distribution** Northern, eastern, and southeastern Australia, including Tasmania; also on New Guinea and many smaller Australasian islands

**Status** Population: abundant. Common and widespread within its range

# Sugar Glider

*Petaurus breviceps*

*The sugar glider is one of Australia's most successful forest marsupials and the local equivalent of the flying squirrels of Europe and North America.*

THE SUGAR GLIDER'S VARIED diet and ability to withstand extreme weather conditions allows it to range from the snowy wooded highlands of Tasmania (where it was introduced in 1835) to the steamy tropical rain forests of northern Queensland and New Guinea.

Looking something like a small squirrel, the sugar glider is one of several gliding members of the possum superfamily. Gliding allows these essentially arboreal animals to move from tree to tree without needing to climb down to ground level, cross the forest floor or open ground, and then laboriously climb the next tree. Not only does it save a lot of time and energy, but it greatly reduces the threat from ground-dwelling predators such as dingoes, foxes, and large lizards.

## The Art of Gliding

Gliding is achieved using two large flaps of skin that extend from wrist to ankle on either side of the animal's body. When the glider leaps into the air with all four legs stretched out wide, the flaps form a parachutelike structure called the patagium. The glider controls its short flights using its fluffy tail as a rudder and by altering the position of the gliding membrane. When coming in to land, the glider swings its back legs forward so that all four feet collide simultaneously with the tree trunk. Each foot is equipped with an opposable toe and five large claws to help grip the tree firmly. From a tall tree a sugar glider can travel an astonishing 160 feet (48 m) in a single leap.

Much of the sugar glider's energy requirements come from the sweet, sticky sap and gum of wattle and eucalyptus trees. However, sugar gliders are true omnivores and will eat all kinds of plant and animal material,

aggressively. Sugar gliders live in groups of up to seven adult animals, plus young. The whole group lives together in a large, leaf-lined nest. In winter the animals huddle together in the nest to keep warm. In exceptionally bad weather they spend much of the day in a deep, energy-saving sleep known as torpor.

The group is dominated by one or two males. As well as fathering all the offspring, the two top-ranking males guard their territory and their females jealously. Scent is important in bonding the group. It is used both for marking territories and each other. Members of the group use individually recognizable scents that are produced in glands on the head, chest, and at the base of the tail. Females have scent glands in their pouch as well.

## Growing Up

Like all marsupials, sugar gliders are born minute, having spent just 16 days inside the mother. After birth the young live for a further two months inside the pouch, emerging for the first time when they are about 70 days old. By nine or 10 months of age they are able to fend for themselves. It is about now that they will usually be driven out of the family territory and must seek a place of their own.

Not surprisingly, independence brings with it many dangers for the young, inexperienced gliders. A large proportion are killed by predators or die of starvation. Some are even killed as a result of injuries sustained in misjudged glides and crash landings.

⊝ *A sugar glider with the patagium extended in flight. Instead of having to climb up and down trees to forage, the animal can simply glide from one to another.*

including seeds, spiders, and insects. The latter are grabbed off leaves and flowers or snatched from flight during a glide.

Good feeding areas and hollow trees for nesting are the key components of good glider habitat. Such places are valuable and defended

**Common name** Leadbeater's possum

**Scientific name** *Gymnobelideus leadbeateri*

**Family** Petauridae

**Order** Diprotodontia

**Size** Length head/body: about 6 in (15 cm); tail length: 6 in (15 cm)

**Weight** 2.5–6 oz (70–170 g)

**Key features** Typical small possum with long, furry tail and large ears; velvety-gray fur marked with dark stripe down back; eyes very large and black; female has front-opening pouch

**Habits** Nocturnal; arboreal; territorial; lives in loose social groups dominated by females

**Breeding** One or 2 young born at any time of year except midsummer after gestation period of 15–17 days. Leaves pouch at 90 days. Weaned at 3 months; sexually mature at 2 years. May live up to 9 years in captivity, 7 in the wild

**Voice** Chattering calls and angry hisses

**Diet** Mostly insects; some sap, gum, and honeydew

**Habitat** Australian mountain ash forests where there is dense wattle acacia undergrowth

**Distribution** Central highlands of Victoria, Australia

**Status** Population: fewer than 5,000; IUCN Endangered. Previously thought to be extinct

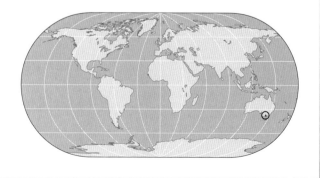

# Leadbeater's Possum

*Gymnobelideus leadbeateri*

*The small Leadbeater's possum was once believed to be extinct, but it has been rediscovered in recent times. However, its habitat requirements are such that future survival seems precarious.*

LEADBEATER'S POSSUM IS REGARDED as a primitive marsupial species. It was first described in 1867, when it was already very rare. The species only lived in forests where there were plenty of old, hollow Australian mountain ash trees in which to nest and a good supply of nearby wattle acacia scrub in which to feed. Elsewhere it was easily outcompeted by more advanced possums, particularly the sugar glider. Leadbeater's possum is relatively unspecialized: It lacks many of the refinements and adaptations shown by other possums, such as an elongated finger for extracting insects from under bark. It also lacks the ability to glide between trees on a web of skin between its front and back limbs.

## Back from the Dead

Changes in climate and vegetation types over the last 2 million years meant that by the late 19th century good habitat for Leadbeater's possum was very hard to find. Only four specimens were recorded before the species apparently disappeared. In 1921, with most of its biology still unknown, it was declared extinct. But in 1961 local wildlife enthusiasts spotted an unfamiliar animal in a stand of regenerating forest in the central highlands of Victoria. Imagine their delight on learning their "mystery animal" was supposed to be extinct!

Further studies revealed a thriving population of Leadbeater's possums benefiting from the aftereffects of a huge wildfire that had devastated the region some 20 years before. The fire had been catastrophic, and huge areas of burned-out habitat were cleared for development or agriculture. The rest was left to

begin the slow but steady process of natural regeneration. Fresh young trees began to grow up around the burned-out remains of the old forest. Luckily, the combination of standing deadwood and vigorous new growth is exactly the kind of habitat favored by Leadbeater's possum. The species was suddenly back in force, taking full advantage of its unexpected second chance and at last giving zoologists an opportunity to study the animals properly.

Leadbeater's possums are nimble climbers and use their tail as a counterbalance when leaping from branch to branch. They are active at night and feed, sleep, and raise their young in the trees. Like other possums, they feed mostly on sap and gum, supplemented with insects deftly caught using their hands.

Unlike most other mammals, the female is the most aggressive. She defends a territory of between 2 and 5 acres (0.8 and 2 ha), aided in the breeding season by her mate and later by her sons. Daughters are driven away as soon as they reach maturity, and many die in the search for a new territory. Most fall victim to predators because they do not have a safe place to hide.

## Uncertain Future

For 20 years the resurrected Leadbeater's possums thrived, but then in the 1980s came signs of a renewed decline. Closer investigation revealed that the dead trees on which the possums depend are collapsing at a rapid rate. Since the rest of the forest is still very young, it will take 100 to 200 years before more old, hollow trees appear to replace them. Unless something is done, the population is destined to crash in the early part of the 21st century. Intensive conservation measures have been put in place to protect the species in nature reserves. Such efforts will have to continue well into the future if the species is not to become extinct for real.

⊕ *The small Leadbeater's possum was rediscovered in the 1960s. However, numbers are declining once again, and the species is now officially classified as Endangered.*

**Common name** Copper ringtail

**Scientific name** *Pseudochirops cupreus*

**Family**     Pseudocheiridae

**Order**      Diprotodontia

**Size**       Length head/body: 14–16 in (35–41 cm); tail length: 10–12 in (26–31 cm)

        **Weight** 3–5 lb (1.4–2.3 kg)

**Key features** Possum with dense, woolly fur that has a coppery sheen; about half the tail is naked and usually held partially curled

**Habits**     Nocturnal; arboreal; normally solitary

**Breeding**  Little known for certain. Probably only 1 young born at a time at any time of year. Gestation, weaning, sexual maturity, and life span unknown

**Voice**     Probably silent most of the time

**Diet**      Generally leaves; also perhaps some fruit

**Habitat**   Mountain forest, mostly above 6,000 ft (2,000 m)

**Distribution** Central highlands of New Guinea

**Status**    Population: abundant. Localized distribution, but apparently plentiful where it occurs

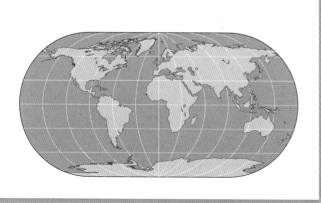

# Copper Ringtail

*Pseudochirops cupreus*

*Like many other mammals of New Guinea, the copper ringtail is fairly numerous and well known to native people. However, virtually no scientific studies of its behavior and ecology have been made.*

THERE ARE ABOUT 15 SPECIES OF ringtails altogether, found mostly in New Guinea, but also in parts of Australia and on some of the nearby islands. Those species that occur in New Guinea, however, are absent from the Australian mainland, and vice versa.

## Coiled Tail

Ringtails are a distinctive group of slow-moving possums closely related to some very ancient evolutionary lines of marsupials. They carry their tails in a coiled ring, hence their name. The hands have five "toes," one or two of which can be folded across the palm to grip food and branches—just as monkeys and humans are able to do. The animals also have a prehensile (gripping) tail that provides additional support when climbing. Such adaptations ensure efficient use of the tree canopy. They enable the ringtails to feed on leaves gathered in the tops of high trees or among the branches of dense shrubs. Like many other tree-dwelling specialists, copper ringtails do not move efficiently on the ground. But they have little to fear from predators, at least in New Guinea where there are no major mammalian predators, apart from human hunters.

The ringtail's teeth are specially adapted to shredding large quantities of tough leaves. The animals also have a voluminous intestine, which is well adapted to dealing with masses of bulky plant food. The copper ringtail is the largest species in the group—about the size of a cat. Its fur has a coppery sheen, again a distinctive feature. Some of the other New Guinea species

**SEE ALSO** Primates **4:**8; Tree Kangaroo, Goodfellow's **10:**66; Cuscus, Spotted **10:**82

*Copper ringtails appear to be among the most abundant medium-sized mammals in the highland forests of New Guinea, a habitat shared by up to three other species of ringtail. The possum has dense, woolly fur with a coppery sheen.*

of ringtail are only known from a few specimens in museums and are probably very rare and restricted in their distribution. The copper ringtail is one of the more numerous ringtail species, occurring throughout the main central highlands of New Guinea.

## Tracked Down by Dogs

The native people of New Guinea traditionally use dogs to hunt mammals for food, catching prey that lives at or near ground level. Despite being a tree-dwelling animal, the copper ringtail often spends the day in a burrow, an unusual habit for an arboreal group of marsupials. Sometimes it is caught asleep in a hollow log or nesting among rocks. A dozen or more may be found and killed in a single day. Indeed, the copper ringtail is one of the most common victims of this type of hunting, and its skull is frequently found among village debris. Yet it is said that the copper ringtail's flesh is not good to eat, perhaps because it is tainted by

distasteful chemicals from the leaves on which it seems to feed. However, copper ringtails are still considered a prize catch because their skins are used in the manufacture of special drums that feature in traditional dances and social gatherings.

There has been a significant loss of forests in parts of lowland New Guinea as a result of logging and forest clearance for agriculture. However, the high-altitude mountain forests where copper ringtails live are less at risk, since it is difficult to extract timber from such steep terrain. Hills at such high elevations also do not make good farmland, so forest clearances tend to be on a small scale. Although the use of shotguns to kill native mammals is now widespread, the nocturnal copper ringtail probably suffers less than more conspicuous animals such as tree kangaroos and cassowaries that can be seen and shot in daylight.

Relatively few copper ringtails have been captured for close examination by scientists, so little is known about the animal's biology. However, pouch young have been reported in many months between January and October, suggesting that the ringtails breed more or less continuously, like many other marsupial species. Again, like many other marsupials, they seem to have only one young at a time. The species would need to breed almost continuously in order to produce sufficient youngsters to compensate for such a small litter size.

# Koala

*Phascolarctos cinereus*

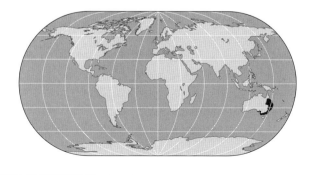

**Common name** Koala (koala bear, native Australian bear)

**Scientific name** *Phascolarctos cinereus*

**Family** Phascolarctidae

**Order** Diprotodontia

**Size** Length head/body: 24–33 in (60–85 cm). Male larger than female; southern koalas larger than northern ones

**Weight** 9–33 lb (4–15 kg)

**Key features** Compact and teddy-bearlike with woolly, grayish-brown fur, paler on belly; large head with round, fluffy ears and large, black nose; tail stumpy; legs longer than they first appear, with 5 large claws on each foot; female has 2 teats in backward-opening pouch

**Habits** Solitary; nocturnal; arboreal; may come to the ground to cross open spaces

**Breeding** Single young (occasionally twins) born September to April (summer) after gestation period of 25–30 days. Leaves pouch after 5–7 months. Weaned at 6–12 months; sexually mature at 2 years. May live up to 20 years in captivity, 18 in the wild

**Voice** Screams, wheezing bellows, and loud wailing associated with courtship and aggression

**Diet** Leaves and bark of various species of eucalyptus trees

**Habitat** Eucalyptus forest and scrub

**Distribution** Eastern Australia

**Status** Population: about 40,000; IUCN Lower Risk: near threatened. Previously hunted for fur and threatened by loss of habitat; now protected and increasing

*The endearing koala used to be hunted for its fur and became quite rare, but strict conservation measures have restored its fortunes. Now there may be too many koalas for small patches of remnant woodland to support.*

AS CUTE, CUDDLY, AND DOCILE as they may appear, koalas are among the world's hardiest animals. What is often mistaken for laziness or a drugged stupor induced by their eucalyptus diet is in fact a highly effective survival strategy. Fossil evidence suggests that koalas evolved about 15 million years ago. It also shows that until 2 million years ago koalas lived in most of the wooded parts of Australia, including the far west, where they now only exist in wildlife parks and as part of introduced populations.

## Regional Differences

The species' range has shrunk, but koala populations are still to be found scattered over a huge area of eastern Australia from temperate Victoria to tropical northern Queensland. Koalas living in the south of the species' range have thicker coats and are up to twice as large as their northern relatives: The extra bulk and insulation help them cope with the chilly winters. Otherwise all koalas look much the same, with a short, teddy-bear face, large black nose, beady black eyes, and rounded ears fringed with white hair.

The koala's coat is dense, woolly, and soft, and in the early part of the 20th century koalas were killed by the million for their highly valued pelts. Today, however, hunting is illegal, and the koala is one of the world's best-loved animals, as well as an Australian national icon.

Sometimes known as the koala bear or native Australian bear, the koala is in fact no such thing. It is a marsupial, and its closest cousins are not bears but wombats. The relationship between koalas and wombats is even more apparent when the koala is seen moving on all fours along the ground. Both species usually walk with a leisurely rolling gait. However, they are capable of bursts of speed when necessary, rapidly covering short distances at a bounding gallop. Even so, koalas are not really at home on the ground and only come down when they need to move from one tree to another. When crossing the forest floor, they move slowly and cautiously. Koalas are strong, steady climbers, and more agile than their normally unhurried movements suggest. Gripping the tree with all four paws, they push with their back legs and haul themselves upward with the front limbs. They then walk steadily along the narrow branches.

## Favorite Trees

Koalas are generally solitary, although in areas of good habitat there may be many individuals living close together. Each adult spends the majority of its time in a few favorite trees within a home range of between 1 and 7 acres (0.4 and 3 ha), depending on the quality of habitat. The

⊕ *A young koala rides on its mother's back. Juveniles continue to travel with their mother for four or five months after leaving the pouch.*

# Funny Feet

**K**oala paws are adapted for grasping. The palms and soles of each hand and foot are hairless, and the skin is rough and granular to enhance grip. Each paw has five clawed toes, but they are arranged differently on the fore- and hind limbs. On the front paws (the koala's "hands") both the first and second digits oppose the other three, rather like having two thumbs. That makes it very easy for the koala to grip branches as it climbs. It also helps when grabbing handfuls of leaves for feeding.

On the hind feet, only the first toe is opposable, and the second is almost completely joined to the third, creating what looks like a single toe with two claws. The so-called syndactylous arrangement of the second and third toes is one of the key features of the large marsupial order Diprotodontia, which contains not only the koala but also the wombats, kangaroos, and possums.

*The koala's large paws are equipped with very sharp, curved claws on most digits. Even when asleep, the animal is able to keep a firm hold.*

home ranges of mature males are larger and overlap with those of several females and subadult males. However, for most of the year the males mind their own business and avoid other koalas, occupying individual trees at different times. But when the summer breeding season arrives, male koalas become aggressive and confrontational. Dominant males patrol their range, evicting smaller males and staking a claim to the resident females with gruff, bellowing calls throughout the night.

### Minute Baby

Females are usually ready to breed at two years old. Male koalas mature at much the same age, but aggressive competition from older, larger males means they rarely get the opportunity to mate until they are at least four years old. After mating the male plays no further part in rearing his offspring. The female is pregnant for just one month before giving birth to a minute baby weighing as little as 0.02 ounces (0.5 g)! The newborn koala is blind and naked, with forelimbs just developed enough to crawl straight into its mother's pouch (a relatively simple journey because the pouch opens backward). Here, it attaches itself securely to one of the two teats with its mouth.

The joey remains in the pouch for the next six months, growing steadily and feeding on

milk whenever it wants to. At about five months it also begins to eat specially predigested eucalyptus leaves in the form of soft droppings, or "pap," produced by its mother. The tough fibers and toxic compounds in the raw leaves are broken down in the mother's gut so the resulting pap is safe to eat and easy to digest. The pap also contains doses of the precious gut-dwelling bacteria that the young koala will need to be able to digest raw eucalyptus leaves in the future.

Once the weaning process has begun, the young koala spends more and more time out of the pouch, riding instead on its mother's back, from where it learns how to feed itself. By about 10 months old it will be ready to begin life on its own; and although it may spend a few more months living close to its mother, it will eventually move on.

Young males tend to travel farther than females in order to escape harassment by older males. Such dispersal journeys are fraught with danger because they require the young, inexperienced koalas to spend more time on the ground than they otherwise would do. Out of the trees the animals are vulnerable to attack by feral and domestic dogs, as well as dingoes. In addition, many are killed by vehicles while trying to cross roads. Once settled, their lives

⊕ *Infant koalas. The koala's appealing teddy-bearlike face has made it one of the world's best-loved animals and an Australian national icon. However, its cute and cuddly appearance belies the fact that it is an extremely hardy creature.*

are relatively safe and uneventful, although many koala populations are afflicted by a disease affecting the eyes caused by bacteria called *Chlamydia psittaci*.

## A Specialized Diet

Koalas feed almost exclusively on the leaves and bark of certain eucalyptus trees. There are over 700 species of eucalyptus in Australia, of which about 20 feature regularly in the diet of koalas. However, none of them can be said to make good eating. Indeed, the leaves of virtually all eucalypts contain a cocktail of unpalatable, indigestible, and downright toxic chemicals. The leaves are also so short of essential nutrients, including nitrogen and phosphorus, that it is

## A Conservation Conundrum

In the early 20th century hunting for fur, habitat destruction by forest fires, and logging threatened the koala with extinction. The species was granted legal protection in 1927 and is once again doing well in many parts of its former range where suitable habitat still exists. However, the patchy nature of the remaining koala habitat is a big problem. Because the koalas in an isolated population respond so well to conservation, their numbers increase rapidly to the point where they begin to damage the very trees they need to survive. Overcrowding leads to starvation, stress, and disease: In many places the

authorities have had to take the drastic and controversial step of culling large numbers of koalas in order to keep the remaining population healthy and disease free. Sometimes the extra koalas can be spared and moved somewhere else; but if conditions are good, they soon outgrow their new home, too. Conservationists are now trying to create corridors of habitat linking isolated patches of trees so that the koala population can disperse as its grows. However, it is an expensive business and not always possible where agriculture and urban development have replaced the original eucalyptus scrub.

amazing any animal should bother with them at all. Yet by specializing in a diet that no other mammal would touch, the cuddly-looking koalas have carved out a comfortable niche for themselves in an otherwise harsh and unforgiving environment.

### Adaptations to Eucalyptus

Getting by on a diet of eucalyptus requires a whole collection of anatomical, physiological, and behavioral adaptations. Anatomically, the koala has efficient grinding teeth, which crush the leaves into a thick paste, breaking down the tough fibrous cell walls and woody tissues before they are swallowed. The koala also has a very long and voluminous gut, which means the food takes a long while to pass through, allowing plenty of time for thorough digestion.

Physiological adaptations to the koala's eucalyptus diet include resistance to some of the toxins in the leaves. Koalas also emit special secretions from the liver and possess bacteria in the gut that help break down and inactivate many indigestible or harmful chemicals. Such chemicals are produced by eucalyptus trees to prevent animals from eating their leaves. Normally, the toxins have the desired effect, since few creatures can eat eucalyptus at all. The koala, on the other hand, eats little else— apart from the occasional mouthful of soil and gravel to help with digestion.

Even allowing for its superefficient digestive system, the koala's diet provides little in the way of energy because it is so low in calories. As a result, the animals rest as much as possible: They are known to spend up to 80 percent of their time asleep—usually securely wedged between the forked branches of a eucalyptus tree. In addition, a substantial proportion of their waking hours is passed in resting. The koala's reputation for being sleepy—even lazy— is actually a behavioral adaptation designed to conserve energy.

⊙ *A koala forages in eucalyptus leaves. The leaves are poisonous to most herbivores, but the koala's liver has adapted to deal with some of the toxins they contain.*

**Common name** Common wombat

**Scientific name** *Vombatus ursinus*

**Family** Vombatidae

**Order** Diprotodontia

**Size** Length head/body: 27.5–47 in (70–120 cm); tail length: 1 in (2.5 cm)

**Weight** 33–77 lb (15–35 kg)

**Key features** Solid, short-legged, bearlike animal with very short tail; large head with short snout, large nose, and small ears; coat of coarse brown fur; long, powerful claws; female has 2 teats in rear-opening pouch

**Habits** Solitary; mostly active at night; digs large burrows

**Breeding** Single young (occasionally twins) mostly born in summer or fall after gestation period of 21 days. Spends a further 2–3 months in pouch. Weaned at 15 months; sexually mature at 2 years. May live up to 26 years in captivity, but fewer in the wild

**Voice** Grunts and abrupt coughing sounds

**Diet** Plant material, including leaves, stems, and roots; also fungi

**Habitat** Forests and scrub in rocky upland areas

**Distribution** Southeastern Australia and Tasmania

**Status** Population: many thousands; IUCN Vulnerable (Flinders Island subspecies). Has declined, but remains secure and common in parts of its geographical range away from human habitation

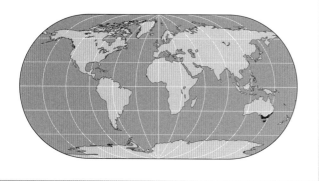

# Common Wombat

*Vombatus ursinus*

*Early European settlers in Australia often referred to wombats as "badgers" because of their similar size, burrowing habits, and nocturnal lifestyle.*

WOMBATS ARE SHORT, THICKSET burrowing animals that look like miniature snub-nosed bears. The name wombat comes from the Aboriginal word for the animal, and the scientific name *ursinus* means "bearlike."

In fact, wombats are not relations of either badgers or bears. They are marsupials, and their closest relative is the koala. The so-called common wombat is decidedly less common now than it was 200 years ago. The animal was once widespread throughout southeastern Australia, including Tasmania and many islands in the Bass Straits. It now has a much more restricted distribution. Of the three recognized subspecies of common wombat, one is now confined to a single island in the Bass Strait; the other two (one on Tasmania, the other on the mainland) are much reduced in range.

## Burrowing Mammals

Wombats are among the world's largest burrowing mammals, and they are superb diggers. They are solidly built animals with short, strong legs adapted for scraping and shoveling soil. Their fur is coarse with little soft underfur, which would clog with dirt. They use their long, powerful claws to loosen soil, which is then scraped aside and kicked back with front and hind legs. Roots and other obstructions to tunneling are attacked using the teeth. Wombats are quite particular about their burrows, with the best sites being well-drained soils close to water, such as in the banks above creeks. If the digging is not going well, the burrow is likely to be abandoned, and most

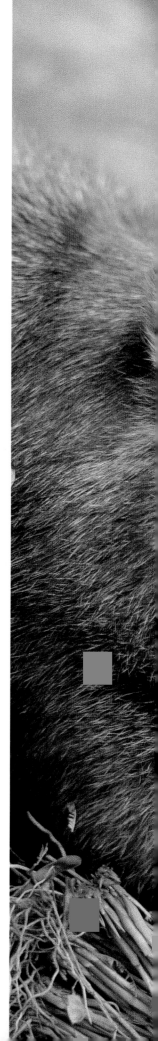

wombat home ranges will include several such half-finished tunnels.

Over time, well-used burrows will be extended. Some are up to 100 feet (30 m) long, with many branching tunnels and several different chambers and entrances. Nest chambers are used for sleeping during the day and contain bedding in the form of grass and stripped bark. There can be dozens of such burrows within a wombat's home range, and the resident animal may visit three or four in the course of a night.

The wombats use regular pathways between burrows and feeding areas, and may travel up to 1.8 miles (3 km) in a night.

## Damaging Habits

Their industrious digging is the main reason why wombats have been intensively hunted ever since people began farming in Australia. The wombat's excavations damage the roots of crops and create hazards for livestock. Cattle and horses are particulary at risk, since a stumble into a burrow often means a broken leg. Usually, such an accident means the injured animal has to be shot. More damaging still is that wombats burrow under fences, thereby giving rabbits access to crops and pastures. Rabbits have been the great scourge of Australian agriculture, and ironically the native wombats have suffered by unwitting association with a species that humans introduced in the first place. Most remaining wombat populations now receive protection, but those in eastern Victoria are still treated as vermin and routinely trapped, shot, and poisoned.

Aside from people, adult wombats have few natural enemies. Young animals are killed by dingoes, eagles, and Tasmanian devils, and probably once fell prey to the thylacine. However, large adults can be aggressive enough to make a predator think twice before attacking. In addition, they have an incredibly thick hide, especially on the rump, so that once inside the entrance to a burrow, they are relatively safe from slashing teeth and claws. From such a position they can deal powerful kicks at the face of their attacker. Much the same technique is used to avoid injury when fighting other wombats, a common activity among males during the breeding season.

Common wombats are solitary and occupy a home range that covers between 7 and 55

⊙ *The wombat's burrowing habits have made it an enemy of local people. Crops can be damaged, and its burrows can be hazardous to livestock.*

*⊕ A common wombat mother and youngster feed on foliage using a fallen log as a dinner table. Wombats are devoted mothers. Their offspring will often follow them around for up to a year after leaving the pouch.*

acres (3 and 22 ha). As a general rule, the resident wombat excludes others—aggressively if need be. However, studies of some populations suggest that is not always the case and that wombats can be quite tolerant of visits from their neighbors. They may even use the same burrows. Wombats personalize their home range using scent marks and droppings deposited on prominent places, such as on logs or rocky outcrops. The droppings are strangely rectangular and easily recognized.

## Attentive Mothers

Female wombats have two mammae (teats), so theoretically they can raise two young. In practice, however, they rarely give birth to more than one baby, on which they lavish devoted attention. The youngster spends three months attached to a teat in the pouch, after which it emerges for increasingly long periods of time. By the time it is 11 months old the youngster will follow its mother when she leaves the burrow to forage, but it still suckles from time to time and is not fully weaned until the age of

# Hairy-Nosed Wombats

There are two other species of wombat in Australia, both in the genus *Lasiorhinus*. These so-called hairy-nosed wombats have a fully furred nose, and their coats are smoother and sleeker than that of the common wombat. Both are adapted to harsher, drier conditions than their common cousin. Another significant difference is that the hairy-nosed wombats live in colonies, with several adults sharing a warren of interconnected burrows.

Life was hard enough for the hairy-nosed wombats before the arrival of European settlers. Both species had apparently undergone a significant decline even before they were properly described by scientists. The northern species (*Lasiorhinus krefftii*) has suffered most seriously, and by 1982 there was just one population of 20 animals left alive—in a national park in central Queensland. Happily, the southern hairy-nosed wombat (*Lasiorhinus latifrons*) has fared a little better.

The northern hairy-nosed wombats have been the subject of a huge conservation effort: They are closely monitored, and cattle are kept well away. The population now consists mostly of young animals, and the prospects for expansion look good. However, the population is dangerously inbred, which is not surprising considering that they are all descended from the same few animals.

about 15 months. A prolonged period of care means that the average female only rears one youngster every two years. Such a slow rate of reproduction means the species is vulnerable to persecution, being unable to rapidly replace animals that are killed.

## Diggers and Foragers

The wombat's digging prowess also serves it well in foraging. It eats mainly grasses, sedges, and fungi. In times of drought roots and underground stems may be the only reliable source of food. It consumes a fair amount of soil and grit with its already tough diet, but a wombat's teeth are well adapted to cope. Like rodents, wombats have just a single pair of incisors, which grow throughout life to compensate for wear at their tips. Even in good times the wombat survives on a relatively poor,

low-energy diet, making the most of every meal by digesting it very slowly. In common with the koala, it has a set of special glands in its stomach that are thought to assist in breaking down tough, sometimes toxic vegetation. Wombats are generally not very lively animals. They are able to run fast when necessary, but as a rule they amble slowly around and spend plenty of time resting and conserving energy. In summer they are almost entirely nocturnal, remaining below ground during the hottest parts of the day in order to conserve water. In winter they may emerge to bask in the sun so that they do not have to expend precious extra energy keeping themselves warm.

⊕ *The southern hairy-nosed wombat has been the subject of huge conservation efforts. The outlook for the species now seems good, but the remaining animals are dangerously inbred.*

## Common name
Honey possum (noolbenger)

**Scientific name** *Tarsipes rostratus*

**Family** Tarsipedidae

**Order** Diprotodontia

**Size** Length head/body: 1.5–4 in (4–9.5 cm); tail length: 2–4 in (4.5–11 cm)

**Weight** 0.2–0.6 oz (7–16 g)

**Key features** Tiny, mouselike marsupial with gray-brown fur marked with 3 dark stripes along the back; long snout and very long tail with hooked, prehensile tip; fingers are long with large, rounded tips and small nails; female has 4 teats in well-developed pouch

**Habits** Nocturnal; arboreal; excellent climber; often gregarious (lives in groups); goes torpid in cold weather

**Breeding** Two to 3 young born at any time of year after gestation period of 21–28 days (plus up to 2 months delayed development in the womb). Leaves pouch at about 4–6 weeks. Weaned at 10 weeks; sexually mature at 10 months. Rarely lives more than 1 year

**Voice** Normally silent

**Diet** Pollen and nectar

**Habitat** Trees and shrubs

**Distribution** Southwestern parts of Western Australia

**Status** Population: unknown, but common where it occurs. Not currently threatened, but may be at risk from loss of habitat

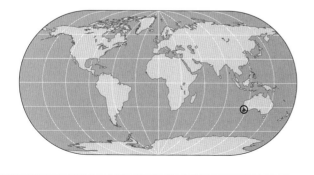

# Honey Possum

*Tarsipes rostratus*

*The tiny honey possum feeds on nectar and pollen taken from flowers. Its unusual diet is shared with a few bats, but almost no other mammals.*

THE HONEY POSSUM IS A UNIQUE animal in many ways. It holds the record for having the smallest babies of any mammal, and yet they arise from the world's longest mammalian sperm! Honey possums are so different from any other kind of living marsupial that they are classified in a separate group from all others. Their closest relative is probably the pygmy possum, but there are so many important differences between the two that some people refuse to call the species a possum at all, preferring the suitably unusual-sounding name "noolbenger."

### Nectar Feeders

Honey possums are among the very few mammals that feed more or less exclusively on pollen and nectar. Their mouths contain very few teeth, most of which are small and peglike and would be useless for chewing or nibbling. By contrast, the tongue is very large—up to a quarter of the animal's whole body length. The tip is very specialized, possessing a brushlike arrangement of hairy projections. The tongue, when combined with the long, narrow snout, can collect pollen direct from flower stamens even when they are hidden deep inside a tubular floret. The pollen is then scraped off the tongue and swallowed. Pollen is very nutritious, and nectar, also taken from the ripe flowers, is almost pure energy-rich sugar. Hence the honey possum has a very efficient diet.

Gaining access to its favorite flowers requires the honey possum to be an extremely agile climber. It grips twigs and stems using its tiny, monkeylike hands and feet (the generic name *Tarsipes* means "tarsier-footed," a reference to the tiny arboreal primate). Each of the five fingers and toes has a round, spreading tip and a short fingernail, except for the second and third toes on the hind feet, which are fused and have larger claws. The long, tapering tail has a flexible, prehensile tip from which the possum can dangle to reach hanging flowers.

## Dominant Females

Honey possums breed almost all year round, with a slight lull in the middle of summer when there is a shortage of pollen. Breeding females tend to live alone, except for their young, but in winter adult animals often gather together to keep warm. If food is scarce, both sexes will undergo short periods of torpor (a deep sleep during which body functions slow right down, and the animal's temperature drops) in order to save energy. Unusually among mammals, female honey possums are socially dominant over males. The largest females in a population jostle for rank and will not share territories, while smaller females and males will live happily together. The honey possum occupies a relatively large home range, within which it will visit different plants as they come into flower. For shelter they use old birds' nests or build their own by using light, dry vegetation.

Breeding is promiscuous and on the female's terms. Males will follow her when she is ready to mate, and she will permit them to approach just long enough to copulate. Unlike many other marsupials, where males grow big in order to compete for females, male honey possums let their outsized sperm do all the competing inside the female. Relatively speaking, male honey possums have the largest testes of any mammal. The young are born after a three- to four-week gestation and weigh about one five thousandth of an ounce (5 mg). After eight weeks in the pouch they have multiplied their weight 500 times, yet still weigh less than a dime (0.1 oz or 2.5 g).

*The minute honey possum uses both its hands and feet to grip twigs and the stems of plants. It is one of very few mammals that feed on nectar and pollen.*

# EGG-LAYING MAMMALS

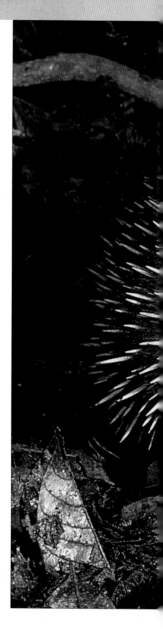

The classification of the animal order Monotremata has puzzled zoologists for two centuries, and even now the matter is not yet fully settled. Although most people accept that monotremes are mammals (because they are furry), for a long time there was a strong move to classify them as reptiles because they lay eggs. Certainly they have more in common with snakes, lizards, and turtles than other mammals do. Some typically "reptilian" characteristics of monotremes include structural features of the eye, skull, and skeleton (especially the bones of the shoulders and hips). Unlike most mammals, the digestive, excretory, and reproductive tracts leave the body via a single opening called the cloaca. This is another typically reptilian arrangement, and gives the group its name: *monotreme* means "one hole."

## Origins

It is tempting to think of the monotremes as a kind of ancestral group, part reptile, part mammal. However, such a theory is simply not borne out by the evidence. It is now believed that monotremes are not ancestors, but simply an independent and separate way of being a mammal. The monotremes (subclass Prototheria) seem to have split from the main branch of the live-bearing mammal (subclass Theria) family tree 125 to 130 million years ago in the Cretaceous period, just before the marsupials (infraclass Metatheria) and placental mammals (infraclass Eutheria) diverged. In evolutionary terms the timescale is really quite recent, considering that the reptile–mammal split may have occured almost twice as long ago in the Triassic period. Monotremes are in fact cousins of other mammals rather than their ancestors.

## Characteristics

The most remarkable feature of monotremes is that—in contrast to all other mammals—they reproduce by laying leathery shelled eggs, just as many reptiles do. During pregnancy the shell is built up around the developing embryo while it is still in the tube connecting the female's ovary to the cloaca. The eggs are incubated and hatched outside the female's body, much as in reptiles and birds.

At one time the breeding details of monotremes seemed an appropriate basis for classifying the platypus and echidnas as an unusual group of reptiles. However, both animals have numerous other characteristics that are most definitely mammalian. For a start, they are warm-blooded— not quite as warm as other mammals perhaps, but still able to keep their body temperature at a fairly constant 86 to 91.4°F (30 to 33°C). They are also hairy, and fur is an exclusively mammalian feature. Most convincing of all, females provide their young with milk secreted by mammary glands. There are no nipples— the milk simply seeps from the glands into the surrounding fur, from where it is lapped up by the babies.

Other characteristics of modern monotremes are the absence of whiskers and external ears. There are also no teeth in adult animals. That is not to say that earlier monotremes were the same. In fact, fossil remains from Australia and South America suggest that earlier platypuslike monotremes had teeth, as do juvenile platypuses today. Whether the animals had ears and whiskers as well is impossible to say because such features are not normally preserved in fossils. Internally, the ears of modern monotremes are much like those of

## Who's Who among the Egg-Laying Mammals? (Subclass Prototheria)

**Family:** Ornithorhynchidae—platypuses: 1 genus, 1 species, duck-billed platypus (*Ornithorhynchus anatinus*)

**Family:** Tachyglossidae—echidnas: 2 genera, 2 species, short-beaked echidna (*Tachyglossus aculeatus*); long-beaked echidna (*Zaglossus bruijni*)

conventional mammals, with three tiny ear bones. The ears of reptiles and birds are quite different.

Monotremes have characteristic spurs on their ankles. In adult male platypuses they are large and sharp and connect to venom glands in the thigh. The spurs are smaller and less obvious in other monotremes, but they are present nonetheless.

*⬆ The long-beaked echidna catches insects on its long tongue at the end of its snout.*

*⬅ An echidna hatches from its soft-shelled egg.*

## Lifestyle

Modern monotremes are confined to the continent of Australia and the island of New Guinea. One species, the short-beaked echidna, is common and widespread owing largely to the fact that it specializes in a diet of ants and termites, for which it has no real competition. The other Australian monotreme, the duck-billed platypus, also has a specialized lifestyle, living close to rivers and pools and catching most of its food underwater. It too faces little competition. The third species, the long-nosed echidna of New Guinea, feeds mainly on worms, which it unearths in humid forests. The animal is heavily reliant on hollow logs, piles of rubble and brush, or thick clumps of vegetation for shelter. Sadly, its habitat is under threat, and the species has been hunted to the brink of extinction by native people.

**Common name** Duck-billed platypus

**Scientific name** *Ornithorhynchus anatinus*

| | |
|---|---|
| **Family** | Ornithorhynchidae |
| **Order** | Monotremata |
| **Size** | Length head/body: 12–18 in (30–45 cm); tail length: 4–6 in (10–15 cm). Male usually larger than female |
| **Weight** | 1–4.4 lb (0.5–2 kg) |

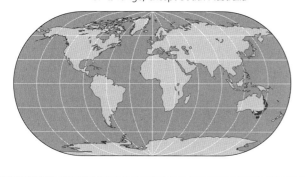

| | |
|---|---|
| **Key features** | Flattened, torpedo-shaped animal with very short legs and large feet, each with 5 webbed toes; snout has soft, rubbery beak with nostrils on top; tail flat and paddlelike; body fur dark brown on back, paler below; male has sharp spurs on ankles |
| **Habits** | Largely aquatic; most active around dusk and dawn; lives in burrows; generally solitary |
| **Breeding** | One to 3 (usually 2) eggs laid after gestation period of 27 days. Young hatch 10 days later and are brooded for a further 4 months in nest burrow. Weaned at 4 months; sexually mature at 2 or 3 years. May live up to 21 years in captivity, 14 in the wild |
| **Voice** | Usually silent; growls if disturbed or annoyed |
| **Diet** | Small aquatic animals, especially crustaceans, insect larvae, worms, fish, and tadpoles |
| **Habitat** | Freshwater streams and pools with suitable burrowing sites along their banks |
| **Distribution** | Eastern Australia, including parts of Tasmania, New South Wales, Victoria, South Australia, and Queensland |
| **Status** | Population: low thousands. Previously hunted for fur, now protected and doing well in most of its range, except South Australia |

# Duck-Billed Platypus

*Ornithorhynchus anatinus*

*With its birdlike bill and egg-laying habits, the platypus is a strange, mixed-up creature. However, it is also extremely well adapted to its way of life.*

THE DUCK-BILLED PLATYPUS IS undoubtedly one of the oddest animals alive today. It is a monotreme—one of a select few mammals that reproduce by laying eggs instead of giving birth to live young. But the peculiarities do not end here. At first glance the platypus appears to be made up of spare parts taken from other animals. The combination of its robust, furry body, huge webbed feet, flat, paddle-shaped tail, and unique rubbery bill seems so unlikely that the first specimen sent back to Europe for scientific description was thought to be a hoax.

## Aquatic Lifestyle

Detailed studies of the duck-billed platypus are hampered by the fact that it is a naturally shy and elusive animal. It spends much of its time hidden away in inconspicuous burrows. When it emerges to feed, usually under cover of twilight, it slips quietly into the cloudy waters of small pools, rivers, and streams and spends much of its time beneath the surface. On land the platypus gets around by waddling. Its large webbed feet, at the end of very short, stumpy legs, are not built for walking but for swimming, which the species does superbly well. Once in the water, it moves smoothly and silently, propelling itself along with its front feet and using the back ones as rudders and brakes. Underwater it moves with the speed and grace of an otter or a seal, able to accelerate rapidly and change direction in an instant. At the surface only the tip of its snout and the top of its head are visible, and it dives suddenly by rolling forward in the water without the tiniest splash. Often the only clue to the animal's presence is the rippling created in the water.

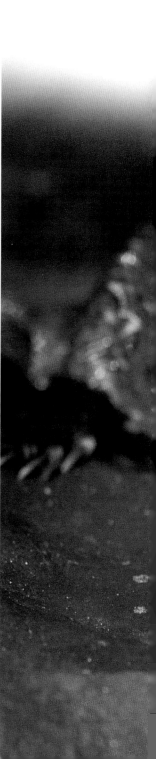

A platypus bill is not really like that of a duck at all. It is, in fact, a finely tuned prey-detection device, sensitive to touch and to the tiny electrical fields generated by the bodies of living animals. Unlike the hard beak of a duck, the bill of a platypus is soft, moist, and rubbery and covered in tiny pits and holes lined with highly sensitive nerve endings that carry information straight to the brain. The platypus also has reasonable eyesight and hearing, but while underwater the bill provides all the information that is required—the eyes and ears are closed while the animal remains submerged. Once detected, prey animals are snapped up or sieved out of the mud using the bill.

After a successful period of foraging a platypus returns to the surface to breathe and feed. Prey items stored in large cheek pouches are brought back into the mouth, crushed and ground between horny plates that line each jaw, and swallowed. It may take several minutes to finish such a meal, during which time the platypus floats easily at the surface with all four legs spreadeagled. The animal looks relaxed, but at the slightest disturbance it will disappear once more.

*The duck-billed platypus appears to be made up of spare parts. Its anatomy seems so unlikely that the first specimen sent to Europe was thought to be a hoax.*

## Venomous Spurs

The platypus is, for the most part, a solitary animal. The home ranges of different individuals may overlap to some extent, but they apparently make an effort to avoid meeting, except during the breeding season. Early in spring male platypuses become very aggressive as they compete for the right to mate with the females living within their range. Fighting is quite common and is a very serious business, despite the platypus's lack of conventional mammalian weapons: The rivals have no teeth with which to bite each other, and their claws are not designed for slashing or scratching. However, each male has a pair of additional clawlike "spurs" growing from the ankles of his hind legs, which point inward and fold down when not in use. In a fight the platypus raises his spurs and tries to spike his opponent. The spurs are connected to glands in the animal's thigh that produce a potent toxin

powerful enough to kill a dog and cause excruciating pain in a human. The male duck-billed platypus is the world's only seriously venomous mammal. All platypus babies have spurs, but they only develop fully in males.

Both male and female platypuses live in burrows in the banks of pools and streams. These general-purpose dens are simple oval tunnels with a sleeping chamber at the end. Breeding females also build nesting burrows, which are much more extensive. Adult platypuses have few natural predators, but the babies are highly vulnerable, so the mother goes to great lengths to build a secure home.

*⬆ The male platypus's poisonous spurs make it the most venomous mammal. Normally, the spurs are folded down to avoid catching on passing objects, but they are erected in a fight between two males.*

## Humid Nests

The nest burrow may extend as far as 65 feet (20 m) into the bank. There can be several twists and turns and blind-ending offshoots. The nest itself is made of damp leaves and other vegetation, which the female collects from the water or the banks. Unlike most other mammals, which do their best to keep nesting areas snug and dry, the atmosphere inside the platypus nest must be humid to prevent the eggs and their precious contents from drying

## Last in Line

The duck-billed platypus is the only surviving member of an ancient family of animals that were once much more widespread. Fossil platypuses dating from the time of the dinosaurs have been found not only in Australia but also in South America, providing strong evidence for the theory that Australia, Antarctica, and South America were once joined together as one supercontinent known as Gondwanaland. Whether or not these animals had anything like the modern platypus's ducklike bill is impossible to say because the bill is made of soft tissue, which does not fossilize. However, these ancient ancestors did have true teeth. The modern platypus only has baby teeth (milk teeth), which are replaced with flat grinding pads made of a horny substance that continues to grow throughout the animal's life. The long-extinct relatives of the duck-billed platypus probably lived mostly on land and fed on small invertebrates, much as generalist insectivores like hedgehogs and shrews do today.

out. Platypus eggs are small—0.7 inches (1.7 cm) in diameter, and rounder than those of most birds. They are sticky enough to stay put in the nest and not roll away. The mother platypus has no pouch in which to incubate her brood; instead, she tucks them safely under her tail and curls around them to keep them warm. Once the eggs hatch, the naked, 1-inch- (2.5-cm-) long babies are cradled in much the same

way. Like a newborn marsupial, a young platypus is little more than an embryo at first—barely able to drag itself along. But it is capable of finding the places on its mother's belly where milk seeps out of her mammary ducts. There are no teats that the young can latch onto, so the babies suck up milk from among the mother's fur. The lack of a pouch means the mother platypus cannot carry her eggs or babies with her. At first she never leaves them alone for more than a few minutes, remaining in the burrow for days at a time. As the young become more able to keep warm, she leaves for longer periods to hunt. However, every time she enters or leaves the burrow, she painstakingly removes and replaces the plugs of earth blocking the tunnels in order to keep the youngsters in and predators out.

⬆ *Ideally adapted for swimming, the duck-billed platypus has a streamlined body with thick, insulating underfur that keeps the animal warm in cold water.*

**Common name** Short-beaked echidna (short-nosed spiny anteater)

**Scientific name** *Tachyglossus aculeatus*

**Family** Tachyglossidae

**Order** Monotremata

**Size** Length head/body: 14–21 in (35–53 cm); tail length: 3.5 in (9 cm)

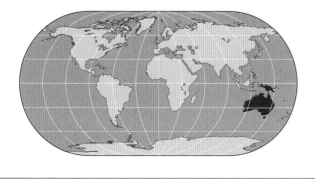

**Weight** 5.5–15.5 lb (2.5–7 kg)

**Key features** Stocky, short-legged animal with domed back covered in thick, dark-brown fur and long, black-tipped yellow spines; large feet have 5 toes with large, blunt claws; tail short; head small with long, whiskerless snout

**Habits** Solitary, but nonterritorial; usually nocturnal; may hibernate in parts of its range; terrestrial, but swims and climbs well; powerful digger

**Breeding** Single egg laid July–August after gestation period of 9–27 days. Incubated in pouchlike fold of skin on mother's belly; hatches after 10 days; spends further 8 weeks in pouch. Weaned at 6–7 months; sexually mature at 1–2 years. May live for over 50 years in captivity, rarely more than 20 in the wild

**Voice** Generally silent

**Diet** Ants and termites

**Habitat** Varied; forest and scrub, open rocky and sandy landscapes; also parks and gardens

**Distribution** Australia, including Tasmania; also New Guinea

**Status** Population: abundant. Common and widespread throughout most of its range

# Short-Beaked Echidna

*Tachyglossus aculeatus*

*The short-beaked echidna, or spiny anteater, is the most common and widespread of the world's three species of egg-laying mammals.*

THE SHORT-BEAKED ECHIDNA IS one of the few native Australian mammals for whom the arrival of European settlers and introduced wildlife has not resulted in a significant decline. By contrast, the long-beaked echidna from New Guinea is currently one of the world's most endangered mammals, mainly owing to habitat loss and hunting by native people.

The short-beaked echidna's success is partly due to its physical characteristics and specialized lifestyle. There is also no doubt that the animal looks very appealing. Since it rarely causes a nuisance to people, it has never suffered any real persecution by humans. Its short, sharp spines are also an effective protection from the various carnivores imported by people to Australia, such as cats, dogs, and foxes. Consequently, echidnas are relatively common animals even in towns and city parks, although being mostly nocturnal, they are rarely seen.

## Spiny Armor

The armory of sharp spines that covers the echidna's back is enough to deter most predators, especially when the animal curls itself into a tight ball. It can also burrow into soft soil so efficiently that it appears to sink vertically into the ground until nothing remains except a few discouraging spikes.

The short-beaked echidna specializes in feeding on ants and termites, which, although abundant, are exploited by relatively few other animals. The echidna's eyes are of little use for feeding purposes and are largely ineffective—the most important sense when it comes to feeding is smell. The echidna shoves its snout into ants' nests and rotten logs, while using its

*⊕ The spines of the short-beaked echidna are longer than those of the long-beaked echidna. In both species fur is present between the spines.*

sticky tongue to lap up the insects. They are mashed a little before swallowing, but the echidna has no teeth, so the "chewing" is done between toughened pads on the tongue and roof of the mouth.

In much of the echidna's range feeding happens at night to avoid the heat of the day. However, in southern parts of Australia daytime feeding excursions in the winter are more common. In very cold winters, such as those in the Snowy Mountains of eastern Australia, echidnas will give up feeding altogether and undergo periods of hibernation.

## Single Young

Except for mothers with young, echidnas live alone. Single animals occupy a home range of between 50 and 500 acres (20 and 200 ha) depending on the type of landscape. The range usually overlaps with those of several other echidnas, but they show little interest in each other except during the breeding season. Males will then seek out females and compete for the opportunity to mate. After mating the male has nothing more to do with the female or the rearing of her young. The female, however, devotes the next seven months to the care of just one baby. She makes a nest in a burrow and lays a single leathery shelled egg about two weeks (or as long as four weeks) after mating. The egg is incubated for a further 10 days in a fold of skin that develops on the female's belly.

The young echidna hatches from the egg with the aid of a special milk tooth, but remains securely cradled in the pouch for many more weeks. Here it has a constant supply of milk, which it laps up directly from the mother's mammary glands that open at pores among her fur.

The young echidna may venture outside the pouch at about three months, but will not be capable of feeding itself until it is about six months old. For a relatively small animal such a long period of dependence is unusual. Compared with the similar-sized rabbit, echidnas breed slowly. But the care lavished on each youngster means that its chances of survival are much higher, and populations are relatively secure.

# List of Species

The following lists all species of marsupials and monotremes:

## Order Didelphimorphia
American opossums

### FAMILY DIDELPHIDAE

#### SUBFAMILY DIDELPHINAE
*Chironectes*
*C. minimus* Water opossum (yapok)
*Didelphis* Large American opossums
*D. albiventris* White-eared opossum
*D. aurita* Big-eared opossum
*D. marsupialis* Southern opossum
*D. virginiana* Virginia or common opossum
*Gracilinanus* Gracile mouse opossums
*G. aceramarcae* Aceramarca gracile mouse
    opossum
*G. agilis* Agile gracile mouse opossum
*G. dryas* Wood spirit gracile mouse opossum
*G. emiliae* Emilia's gracile mouse opossum
*G. marica* Northern or Venezuelan gracile mouse
    opossum
*G. microtarsus* Brazilian or small-footed gracile
    mouse opossum
*Lestodelphys*
*L. halli* Patagonian opossum
*Lutreolina*
*L. crassicaudata* Lutrine opossum (thick-tailed water
    opossum)
*Marmosa* Mouse opossums
*M. andersoni* Anderson's mouse opossum
*M. canescens* Grayish mouse opossum
*M. lepida* Little rufous mouse opossum
*M. mexicana* Mexican mouse opossum
*M. murina* Murine or common mouse opossum
*M. robinsoni* Robinson's or pale-bellied mouse
    opossum
*M. rubra* Red mouse opossum
*M. tyleriana* Tyler's mouse opossum
*M. xerophila* Dryland mouse opossum
*Marmosops* Slender mouse opossums
*M. cracens* Slim-faced slender mouse opossum
*M. dorothea* Dorothy's slender mouse opossum
*M. fuscatus* Gray-bellied slender mouse opossum
*M. handleyi* Handley's slender mouse opossum
*M. impavidus* Andean slender mouse opossum
*M. incanus* Gray slender mouse opossum
*M. invictus* Slaty slender mouse opossum
*M. noctivagus* White-bellied slender mouse
    opossum
*M. parvidens* Delicate slender mouse opossum
*Metachirus*
*M. nudicaudatus* Brown "four-eyed" opossum
*Micoureus* Woolly mouse opossums
*M. alstoni* Alston's woolly mouse opossum
*M. constantiae* Pale-bellied woolly mouse opossum
*M. demerarae* Long-furred woolly mouse opossum
*M. regina* Short-furred woolly mouse opossum
*Monodelphis* Short-tailed opossums
*M. adusta* Sepia or cloudy short-tailed opossum
*M. americana* Three-striped short-tailed opossum
*M. brevicaudata* Red-legged short-tailed opossum
*M. dimidiata* Southern short-tailed opossum
*M. domestica* Gray short-tailed opossum
*M. emiliae* Emilia's short-tailed opossum
*M. iheringi* Ihering's short-tailed opossum
*M. kunsi* Pygmy or Kuns' short-tailed opossum
*M. maraxina* Marajo short-tailed opossum
*M. osgoodi* Osgood's short-tailed opossum
*M. rubida* Chestnut-striped short-tailed opossum
*M. scalops* Long-nosed short-tailed opossum
*M. sorex* Shrewish short-tailed opossum
*M. theresa* Theresa's short-tailed opossum
*M. unistriata* One-striped short-tailed opossum
*Philander* Gray and black "four-eyed" opossums
*P. andersoni* Black "four-eyed" opossum
*P. opossum* Gray "four-eyed" opossum
*Thylamys* Fat-tailed opossums
*T. elegans* Elegant fat-tailed opossum
*T. macrura* Long-tailed fat-tailed opossum
*T. pallidior* Pallid fat-tailed opossum

*T. pusilla* Small fat-tailed opossum
*T. velutinus* Velvety fat-tailed opossum

#### SUBFAMILY CALUROMYINAE
*Caluromys* Woolly opossums
*C. derbianus* Central American or Derby's woolly
    opossum
*C. lanatus* Western or Ecuadorian woolly opossum
*C. philander* Bare-tailed woolly opossum
*Caluromysiops*
*C. irrupta* Black-shouldered opossum
*Glironia*
*G. venusta* Bushy-tailed opossum

## Order Paucituberculata
Shrew or rat opossums

### FAMILY CAENOLESTIDAE

*Caenolestes* Northern shrew opossums
*C. caniventer* Gray-bellied shrew opossum
*C. convelatus* Blackish shrew opossum
*C. fuliginosus* Silky shrew opossum
*Lestoros*
*L. inca* Incan or Peruvian shrew opossum
*Rhyncholestes*
*R. raphanurus* Chilean shrew opossum

## Order Microbiotheria

### FAMILY MICROBIOTHERIIDAE

*Dromiciops*
*D. gliroides/australis* Monito del Monte (colocolos)

## Order Dasyuromorphia
Australasian carnivorous marsupials

### FAMILY DASYURIDAE
Dasyurids

*Antechinomys*
*A. laniger* Kultarr
*Antechinus* Antechinuses
*A. bellus* Fawn antechinus
*A. flavipes* Yellow-footed antechinus
*A. godmani* Atherton antechinus
*A. leo* Cinnamon antechinus
*A. melanurus* Black-tailed antechinus
*A. minimus* Swamp antechinus
*A. naso* Long-nosed antechinus
*A. stuartii* Brown antechinus
*A. swainsonii* Dusky antechinus
*A. wilhelmina* Lesser antechinus
*Dasycercus* Crested-tailed marsupial mice
*D. byrnei* Kowari
*D. cristicauda* Mulgara
*D. hilleri* Ampurta
*Dasykaluta*
*D. rosamondae* Little red kaluta
*Dasyurus* Quolls
*D. albopunctatus* New Guinean quoll
*D. geoffroii* Western quoll
*D. hallucatus* Northern quoll
*D. maculatus* Spotted-tailed or tiger quoll
*D. spartacus* Bronze quoll
*D. viverrinus* Eastern quoll
*Murexia* Long-tailed dasyures
*M. longicaudata* Short-furred dasyure
*M. rothschildi* Broad-striped dasyure
*Myoictis*
*M. melas* Three-striped marsupial mouse
*Neophascogale*
*N. lorentzi* Long-clawed marsupial mouse (speckled
    dasyure)
*Ningaui* Ningauis
*N. ridei* Wongai or inland ningaui
*N. timealeyi* Pilbara ningaui
*N. yvonnae* Southern ningaui
*Parantechinus* Dibblers

*P. apicalis* Dibbler (southern dibbler)
*P. bilarni* Sandstone dibbler
*Phascogale* Phascogales
*P. calura* Red-tailed phascogale (wambenger)
*Phascolosorex* Marsupial shrews
*P. doriae* Red-bellied dasyure
*P. dorsalis* Narrow-striped dasyure
*Planigale* Planigales
*P. gilesi* Paucident planigale
*P. ingrami* Long-tailed planigale
*P. maculata* Pygmy or common planigale
*P. novaeguineae* Papuan or New Guinean planigale
*P. tenuirostris* Narrow-nosed planigale
*Pseudantechinus* Pseudantechinuses
*P. macdonnellensis* Fat-tailed pseudantechinus
*P. ningbing* Ningbing pseudantechinus
*P. woolleyae* Woolley's pseudantechinus
*Sarcophilus*
*S. harrisii (laniarius)* Tasmanian devil
*Sminthopsis* Dunnarts
*S. aitkeni* Kangaroo Island dunnart
*S. archeri* Chestnut dunnart
*S. butleri* Carpentarian dunnart
*S. crassicaudata* Fat-tailed dunnart
*S. dolichura* Little long-tailed dunnart
*S. douglasi* Julia Creek dunnart
*S. fuliginosus* Sooty dunnart
*S. gilberti* Gilbert's dunnart
*S. granulipes* White-tailed dunnart
*S. griseoventer* Gray-bellied dunnart
*S. hirtipes* Hairy-footed dunnart
*S. leucopus* White-footed dunnart
*S. longicaudata* Long-tailed dunnart
*S. macroura* Stripe-faced dunnart
*S. murina* Slender-tailed dunnart
*S. ooldea* Ooldea dunnart
*S. psammophila* Sandhill dunnart
*S. virginiae* Red-cheeked dunnart
*S. youngsoni* Lesser hairy-footed dunnart

### FAMILY THYLACINIDAE

*Thylacinus*
*T. cynocephalus* Thylacine (Tasmanian wolf or tiger)
    Extinct

### FAMILY MYRMECOBIIDAE

*Myrmecobius*
*M. fasciatus* Numbat (banded anteater)

## Order Peramelemorphia
Bandicoots and bilbies

### FAMILY PERAMELIDAE
Australian Bandicoots and bilbies

*Chaeropus*
*C. ecaudatus* Pig-footed bandicoot
*Isoodon* Short-nosed bandicoots
*I. auratus* Golden bandicoot
*I. macrourus* Northern brown bandicoot
*I. obesulus* Southern brown bandicoot (quenda)
*Macrotis* Bilbies
*M. lagotis* Greater bilby
*M. leucura* Lesser bilby
*Perameles* Long-nosed bandicoots
*P. bougainville* Western barred bandicoot
*P. eremiana* Desert bandicoot
*P. gunnii* Eastern barred bandicoot
*P. nasuta* Long-nosed bandicoot

### FAMILY PERORYCTIDAE
Rainforest bandicoots

*Echymipera* Echymiperas
*E. clara* Clara's echymipera
*E. davidi* David's echymipera
*E. echinista* Menzie's echymipera
*E. kalubu* Kalubu echymipera
*E. rufescens* Rufous spiny bandicoot (long-nosed
    echymipera)
*Microperoryctes* Mouse bandicoots

*M. longicauda* Striped bandicoot
*M. murina* Mouse bandicoot
*M. papuensis* Papuan bandicoot
**Peroryctes** New Guinean bandicoots
*P. broadbenti* Giant bandicoot
*P. raffrayana* Raffray's bandicoot
**Rhynchomeles**
*R. prattorum* Seram bandicoot

## Order Notoryctemorphia
Marsupial moles

### FAMILY NOTORYCTIDAE

*Notoryctes*
*N. caurinus* Northwestern marsupial mole
*N. typhlops* Marsupial mole

## Order Diprotodontia
Koala, wombats, possums, kangaroos, and relatives

### FAMILY PHALANGERIDAE
Cuscuses and brushtail possums

*Ailurops*
*A. ursinus* Bear cuscus
**Phalanger** Cuscuses
*P. carmelitae* Mountain cuscus
*P. intercastellanus* Southern common cuscus
*P. lullulae* Woodlark Island cuscus
*P. matanim* Telefomin cuscus
*P. orientalis* Gray cuscus
*P. ornatus* Moluccan cuscus
*P. rothschildi* Obi Island cuscus
*P. sericeus* Silky cuscus
*P. gymnotis* Ground cuscus
*P. vestitus* Stein's cuscus
**Spilocuscus** Spotted cuscuses
*S. kraemeri* Admiralty cuscus
*S. maculatus* Short-tailed spotted cuscus
*S. papuensis* Waigeon cuscus
*S. rufoniger* Black-spotted cuscus
**Strigocuscus** Plain cuscuses
*S. celebensis* Little Celebes cuscus
*S. pelengensis* Peleng Island cuscus
**Trichosurus** Brushtail possums
*T. caninus* Mountain brushtail possum
*T. vulpecula* Silver gray brushtail possum
**Wyulda**
*W. squamicaudata* Scaly-tailed possum

### FAMILY PSEUDOCHEIRIDAE
Ringtail possums

*Hemibelideus*
*H. lemuroides* Brush-tipped ringtail possum
**Petauroides**
*P. volans* Greater glider
**Petropseudes**
*P. dahli* Rock ringtail possum
**Pseudocheirus**
*P. occidentalis* Western ringtail possum
*P. peregrinus* Common ringtail
**Pseudochirulus**
*P. canescens* Lowland ringtail (Daintree River ringtail)
*P. caroli* Weyland ringtail
*P. cinereus* Daintree River ringtail possum
*P. forbesi* Moss-forest ringtail
*P. herbertensis* Herbert River ringtail
*P. mayeri* Pygmy ringtail
*P. schlegeli* Arfak ringtail
**Pseudochirops**
*P. albertisii* D'Albertis' ringtail possum
*P. archeri* Green ringtail possum
*P. corinnae* Plush-coated or golden ringtail possum
*P. cupreus* Copper ringtail possum

### FAMILY PETAURIDAE
Gliding and striped possums

*Dactylopsila* Striped possums
*D. megalura* Great-tailed triok

*D. palpator* Long-fingered triok
*D. tatei* Tate's triok
*D. trivirgata* Striped possum
**Gymnobelideus**
*G. leadbeateri* Leadbeater's possum
**Petaurus** Lesser gliding possums
*P. abidi* Northern glider
*P. australis* Fluffy or yellow-bellied glider
*P. biacensis* Black glider
*P. breviceps* Sugar glider
*P. gracilis* Mahogany glider
*P. norfolcensis* Squirrel glider

### FAMILY BURRAMYIDAE
Pygmy possums

*Burramys*
*B. parvus* Mountain pygmy possum
**Cercartetus** Pygmy possums
*C. caudatus* Long-tailed pygmy possum
*C. concinnus* Western pygmy possum
*C. lepidus* Tasmanian pygmy possum
*C. nanus* Eastern pygmy possum

### FAMILY ACROBATIDAE
Feathertail gliders and possums

*Acrobates*
*A. pygmaeus* Feathertail glider
**Distoechurus**
*D. pennatus* Feathertail possum

### FAMILY TARSIPEDIDAE

*Tarsipes*
*T. rostratus* Honey possum

### FAMILY PHASCOLARCTIDAE

*Phascolarctos*
*P. cinereus* Koala

### FAMILY VOMBATIDAE
Wombats

*Lasiorhinus* Hairy-nosed wombats
*L. krefftii* Northern or Queensland hairy-nosed wombat
*L. latifrons* Southern hairy-nosed or plains wombat
**Vombatus**
*V. ursinus* Coarse-haired, common, forest, or naked-nosed wombat

### FAMILY HYPSIPRYMNODONTIDAE

*Hypsiprymnodon*
*H. moschatus* Musky rat-kangaroo

### FAMILY MACROPODIDAE

#### SUBFAMILY STHENURINAE
*Lagostrophus*
*L. fasciatus* Banded hare wallaby (munning)

#### SUBFAMILY POTOROINAE
Bettongs, Rat-kangaroos, and potoroos
*Aepyprymnus*
*A. rufescens* Rufous rat-kangaroo
**Bettongia** Bettongs
*B. gaimardi* Tasmanian or Gaimard's bettong
*B. lesueur* Burrowing or Lesueur's bettong (boodie)
*B. penicillata* Brush-tailed bettong (woylie)
*B. tropica* Northern bettong
**Caloprymnus**
*C. campestris* Desert rat-kangaroo
**Potorous** Potoroos
*P. longipes* Long-footed potoroo
*P. platyops* Broad-faced potoroo Extinct
*P. tridactylus* Long-nosed potoroo

#### SUBFAMILY MACROPODINAE
Kangaroos and wallabies
*Dendrolagus* Tree kangaroos
*D. bennettianus* Bennett's tree kangaroo
*D. dorianus* Doria's, dusky, or unicolored tree kangaroo

*D. goodfellowi* Goodfellow's or ornate tree kangaroo
*D. inustus* Grizzled tree kangaroo
*D. lumholtzi* Lumholtz's tree kangaroo
*D. matschiei* Huon or Matschie's tree kangaroo
*D. mbaiso* Dingiso
*D. scottae* Tenkile tree kangaroo
*D. spadix* Lowland tree kangaroo
*D. ursinus* White-throated tree kangaroo
**Dorcopsis** Dorcopsises
*D. atrata* Black dorcopsis
*D. hageni* White-striped dorcopsis
*D. luctuosa* Gray dorcopsis
*D. muelleri* Brown dorcopsis
**Dorcopsulus** Forest wallabies
*D. macleayi* Papuan or Macleay's forest wallaby
*D. vanheurni* Lesser forest wallaby
**Lagorchestes** Hare wallabies
*L. asomatus* Central hare wallaby Extinct
*L. conspicillatus* Spectacled hare wallaby
*L. hirsutus* Western or rufous hare wallaby
*L. leporides* Eastern hare wallaby Extinct
**Macropus** Wallabies, wallaroos, and kangaroos
*M. agilis* Agile wallaby
*M. antilopinus* Antilopine wallaroo
*M. bernardus* Black wallaroo
*M. dorsalis* Black-striped wallaby
*M. eugenii* Tammar or scrub wallaby
*M. fuliginosus* Western gray or black-faced kangaroo
*M. giganteus* Eastern gray or great gray kangaroo
*M. greyi* Toolache wallaby Extinct
*M. irma* Western brush wallaby
*M. parma* Parma or white-fronted wallaby
*M. parryi* Whiptail or Parry's wallaby
*M. robustus* Common or hill wallaroo
*M. rufogriseus* Red-necked wallaby
*M. rufus* Red kangaroo
**Onychogalea** Nail-tailed wallabies
*O. fraenata* Bridled nail-tailed wallaby
*O. lunata* Crescent nail-tailed wallaby
*O. unguifera* Northern nail-tailed wallaby
**Petrogale** Rock wallabies
*P. assimilis* Allied rock wallaby ·
*P. brachyotis* Short-eared rock wallaby
*P. burbidgei* Burbridge's rock wallaby (monjon)
*P. coenensis* Cape York rock wallaby
*P. concinna* Pygmy rock wallaby (nabarlek)
*P. godmani* Godman's rock wallaby
*P. inornata* Unadorned rock wallaby
*P. lateralis* Black-footed rock wallaby
*P. penicillata* Brush-tailed rock wallaby
*P. persephone* Proserpine rock wallaby
*P. rothschildi* Rothschild's rock wallaby
*P. sharmani* Mount Claro rock wallaby
*P. xanthopus* Yellow-footed rock wallaby
**Setonix**
*S. brachyurus* Quokka
**Thylogale** Pademelons
*T. billardierii* Tasmanian pademelon
*T. brunii* Dusky pademelon
*T. stigmatica* Red-legged pademelon
*T. thetis* Red-necked pademelon
**Wallabia**
*W. bicolor* Swamp wallaby

## Order Monotremata
Monotremes

### FAMILY ORNITHORHYNCHIDAE

*Ornithorhynchus*
*O. anatinus* Duck-billed platypus

### FAMILY TACHYGLOSSIDAE

*Tachyglossus*
*T. aculeatus* Short-beaked echidna (common echidna, spiny anteater)

*Zaglossus*
*Z. bruijni* Long-beaked echidna (long-nosed echidna, spiny anteater)

# Glossary

Words in SMALL CAPITALS refer to other entries in the glossary.

**Adaptation** features of an animal that adjust it to its environment; may be produced by evolution—e.g., camouflage coloration

**Adaptive radiation** when a group of closely related animals (e.g., members of a FAMILY) have evolved differences from each other so that they can survive in different NICHES

**Adult** a fully grown animal that has reached breeding age

**Anal gland** (anal sac) a gland opening by a short duct either just inside the anus or on either side of it

**Arboreal** living among the branches of trees

**Arthropod** animals with a jointed outer skeleton, e.g., crabs and insects

**Biodiversity** a variety of SPECIES and the variation within them

**Biomass** the total weight of living material

**Biped** any animal that walks on two legs. See QUADRUPED

**Breeding season** the entire cycle of reproductive activity from courtship, pair formation (and often establishment of TERRITORY), through nesting to independence of young

**Browsing** feeding on leaves of trees and shrubs

**Cache** a hidden supply of food; also (verb) to hide food for future use

**Callosities** hardened, thickened areas on the skin (e.g., ischial callosities in some PRIMATES)

**Canine** (tooth) a sharp stabbing tooth usually longer than rest

**Cannon bone** a bone formed by fusion of metatarsal bones in the feet of some FAMILIES

**Canopy** continuous (closed) or broken (open) layer in forests produced by the intermingling of branches of trees

**Capillaries** tiny blood vessels that convey blood through organs from arteries to veins

**Carnassial** (teeth) opposing pair of teeth especially adapted to shear with a cutting (scissorlike) edge; in living mammals the arrangement is unique to Carnivora and the teeth involved are the fourth upper PREMOLAR and first lower MOLAR

**Carnivore** meat-eating animal

**Carrion** dead animal matter used as a food source by scavengers

**Cecum** a blind sac in the digestive tract, opening out from the junction between the small and large intestines. In herbivorous mammals it is often very large; it is the site of bacterial action on CELLULOSE. The end of the cecum is the appendix; in SPECIES with a reduced cecum the appendix may retain an antibacterial function

**Cellulose** the material that forms the cell walls of plants

**Cementum** hard material that coats the roots of mammalian teeth. In some SPECIES cementum is laid down in annual layers that, under a microscope, can be counted to estimate the age of individuals

**Cheek pouch** a pockey inside the mouth used for the temporary storage of food,

**Cheek teeth** teeth lying behind the CANINES in mammals, consisting of PREMOLARS and MOLARS

**CITES** Convention on International Trade in Endangered Species. An agreement between nations that restricts international trade to permitted levels through a system of licensing and administrative controls. Rare animals and plants are assigned to categories: (for instance Appendix 1, 2). See Volume 1 page 11

**Cloaca** cavity in the pelvic region into which the gut, reproductive, and urinary ducts open. The cloaca forms a single opening to the body instead of a separate anus and openings for sexual and excretory activities

**Cloven hoof** foot that is formed from two toes, each within a horny covering

**Congenital** condition animal is born with

**Coniferous forest** evergreen forests found in northern regions and mountainous areas dominated by pines, spruces, and cedars

**Corm** underground food storage bulb of certain plants

**Cursorial** adapted for running

**Deciduous forest** dominated by trees that lose their leaves in winter (or the dry season)

**Deforestation** the process of cutting down and removing trees for timber or to create open space for activities such as growing crops and grazing animals

**Delayed implantation** when the development of a fertilized egg is suspended for a variable period before it implants into the wall of the UTERUS and completes normal pregnancy. Births are thus delayed until a favorable time of year, giving the young a better chance of survival

**Den** a shelter, natural or constructed, used for sleeping, giving birth, and raising young; act (verb) of retiring to a den to give birth and raise young or for winter shelter

**Dental formula** a convention for summarizing the dental arrangement, in which the numbers of all types of tooth in each half of the upper and lower jaw are given. The numbers are always presented in the order: INCISOR (I), CANINE (C), PREMOLAR (P), MOLAR (M). The final figure is the total number of teeth to be found in the skull. A typical example for Carnivora would be I3/3, C1/1, P4/4, M3/3 = 44

**Dentition** an animal's set of teeth

**Desert** area of low rainfall dominated by specially adapted plants such as cacti

**Diapause** see DELAYED IMPLANTATION

**Diastema** space between teeth, usually the INCISORS and CHEEK TEETH. It is typical of rodents and lagomorphs, although also found in UNGULATES

**Digit** a finger or toe

**Digitigrade** method of walking on the toes without the heel touching the ground. See PLANTIGRADE

**Dispersal** the scattering of young animals going to live away from where they were born and brought up

**Display** any relatively conspicuous pattern of behavior that conveys specific information to others, usually to members of the same SPECIES; can involve visual or vocal elements, as in threat, courtship, or greeting displays

**Diurnal** active during the day

**DNA** (deoxyribonucleic acid) the substance that makes up the main part of the chromosomes of all living things; contains the genetic code that is handed down from generation to generation

**Domestication** process of taming and breeding animals to provide help and useful products for humans

**Dormancy** a state in which—as a result of hormone action—growth is suspended and metabolic activity reduced to a minimum

**Dorsal** relating to the back or spinal part of the body; usually the upper surface

**Droppings** see FECES and SCATS

**Ecosystem** a whole system in which plants, animals, and their environment interact

**Edentate** toothless, but is also used as group name for anteaters, sloths, and armadillos

**Endemic** found only in one small geographical area, nowhere else

**Estivation** inactivity or greatly decreased activity in hot or dry weather

**Estrus** the period when eggs are released from the female's ovaries, and she becomes available for successful mating. Estrous females are often referred to as "in heat" or as "RECEPTIVE" to males

**Eutherian** mammals that give birth to babies, not eggs, and rear them without using a pouch on the mother's belly

**Extinction** process of dying out in which every last individual dies, and the SPECIES is lost forever

**Family** technical term for a group of closely related SPECIES that often also look quite similar. Zoological family names always end in "idae." See Volume 1 page 11. Also a social group within a species consisting of parents and their offspring

**Feces** remains of digested food expelled from body as pellets, often with SCENT secretions

**Feral** domestic animals that have gone wild and live independently of people

**Flystrike** where CARRION-feeding flies have laid their eggs on an animal

**Fossorial** adapted for digging and living in burrows or underground tunnels

**Frugivore** an animal that eats fruit as main part of the diet

**Fur** mass of hairs forming a continuous coat characteristic of mammals

**Fused** joined together

**Gene** the basic unit of heredity enabling one generation to pass on characteristics to its offspring

**Generalist** an animal that is capable of a wide range of activities, not specialized

**Genus** a group of closely related SPECIES. The plural is genera. See Volume 1 page 11

**Gestation** the period of pregnancy between fertilization of the egg and birth of the baby

**Grazing** feeding on grass

**Gregarious** living together in loose groups or herds

**Harem** a group of females living in the same TERRITORY and consorting with a single male

**Herbivore** an animal that eats plants (grazers and browsers are thus herbivores)

**Heterodont** DENTITION specialized into CANINES, INCISORS, and PREMOLARS, each type of tooth having a different function. See HOMODONT

**Hibernation** becoming inactive in winter, with lowered body temperature to save energy. Hibernation takes place in a special nest or DEN called a hibernaculum

**Homeothermy** maintenance of a high and constant body temperature by means of internal processes; also called "warm-blooded"

**Home range** the area that an animal uses in the course of its normal periods of activity. See TERRITORY

**Homodont** DENTITION in which the teeth are all similar in appearance and function

**Hybrid** offspring of two closely related SPECIES that can breed, but the hybrid is sterile and so cannot produce young

**Inbreeding** breeding among closely related animals (e.g., cousins) leading to weakened genetic composition and reduced survival rates

**Incisor** (teeth) simple pointed teeth at the front of the jaws used for nipping and snipping

**Indigenous** living naturally in a region; NATIVE (i.e., not an introduced SPECIES)

**Insectivore** animals that feed on insects and similar small prey. Also used as a group name for animals such as hedgehogs, shrews, and moles

**Interbreeding** breeding between animals of different SPECIES or varieties within a single FAMILY or strain; interbreeding can cause dilution of the gene pool

**Interspecific** between SPECIES

**Intraspecific** between individuals of the same SPECIES

**Invertebrates** animals that have no backbone (or other true bones) inside their body, e.g., mollusks, insects, and jellyfish

**IUCN** International Union for the Conservation of Nature, responsible for assigning animals and plants to internationally agreed categories of rarity. See table below

**Joey** a young kangaroo living in its mother's pouch

**Juvenile** a young animal that has not yet reached breeding age

**Keratin** tough, fibrous material that forms hairs, feathers, and protective plates on the skin of VERTEBRATE animals

**Lactation** process of producing milk in MAMMARY GLANDS for offspring

**Larynx** voice box where sounds are created

**Latrine** place where FECES are left regularly, often with SCENT added

**Leptospirosis** disease caused by leptospiral bacteria in kidneys and transmitted via urine

**Mammary glands** characteristic of mammals, glands for production of milk

**Marine** living in the sea

**Matriarch** senior female member of a social group

**Metabolic rate** the rate at which chemical activities occur within animals, including the exchange of gasses in respiration and the liberation of energy from food

**Metabolism** the chemical activities within animals that turn food into energy

**Migration** movement from one place to another and back again, usually seasonal

**Molars** large crushing teeth at the back of the mouth

**Molt** the process in which mammals shed hair, usually seasonal

**Monogamous** animals that have only one mate at a time

**Monotreme** egg-laying mammal, e.g., platypus, echidna

**Montane** in a mountain environment

**Musk** mammalian SCENT

**Mutation** random changes in genetic material

## IUCN CATEGORIES

**EX Extinct**, when there is no reasonable doubt that the last individual of a species has died.

**EW Extinct in the Wild**, when a species is known only to survive in captivity or as a naturalized population well outside the past range.

**CR Critically Endangered**, when a species is facing an extremely high risk of extinction in the wild in the immediate future.

**EN Endangered**, when a species faces a very high risk of extinction in the wild in the near future.

**VU Vulnerable**, when a species faces a high risk of extinction in the wild in the medium-term future.

**LR Lower Risk**, when a species has been evaluated and does not satisfy the criteria for CR, EN, or VU.

**DD Data Deficient**, when there is not enough information about a species to assess the risk of extinction.

**NE Not Evaluated**, species that have not been assessed by the IUCN criteria.

**Native** belonging to that area or country, not introduced by human assistance

**Natural selection** when animals and plants are challenged by natural processes (including predation and bad weather) to ensure survival of the fittest

**New World** the Americas; OLD WORLD refers to the non-American continents (not usually Australia)

**Niche** part of a habitat occupied by an ORGANISM, defined in terms of all aspects of its lifestyle

**Nocturnal** active at night

**Nomadic** animals that have no fixed home, but wander continuously

**Old World** non-American continents. See NEW WORLD

**Olfaction** sense of smell

**Omnivore** an animal that eats almost anything, meat or vegetable

**Opportunistic** taking advantage of every varied opportunity that arises; flexible behavior

**Opposable** fingers or toes that can be brought to bear against others on the same hand or foot in order to grip objects

**Order** a subdivision of a class of animals, consisting of a series of related animal FAMILIES. See Volume 1 page 11

**Organism** any member of the animal or plant kingdom; a body that has life

**Oviparous** producing eggs that hatch outside the body of the mother (in fish, reptiles, birds, and MONOTREMES)

**Ovulation** release of egg from the female's ovary prior to its fertilization

**Pair bond** behavior that keeps a male and a female together beyond the time it takes to mate; marriage is a "pair bond"

**Parasite** an animal or plant that lives on or in body of another

**Parturition** process of giving birth

**Pelage** furry coat of a mammal

**Pelagic** living in upper waters of the open sea or large lakes

**Pheromone** SCENT produced by animals to enable others to find and recognize them

**Physiology** the processes and workings within plants and animal bodies, e.g., digestion. Keeping a warm-blooded state is a part of mammal physiology

**Placenta** the structure that links an embryo to its mother during pregnancy, allowing exchange of chemicals between them

**Placental mammal** see EUTHERIAN

**Plantigrade** walking on soles of the feet with heels touching the ground. See DIGITIGRADE

**Polygamous** when animals have more than one mate in a single mating season

**Polygynous** when a male mates with several females in one BREEDING SEASON

**Population** a distinct group of animals of the same SPECIES or all the animals of that species

**Posterior** the hind end or behind another structure

**Predator** an animal that kills live prey for food

**Prehensile** grasping tail or fingers

**Premolars** teeth found in front of MOLARS, but behind CANINES

**Primate** a group of mammals that includes monkeys, apes, and ourselves

**Promiscuous** mating often with many mates, not just one

**Protein** chemicals made up of amino acids. Essential in the diet of animals

**Quadruped** an animal that walks on all fours (a BIPED walks on two legs)

**Range** the total geographical area over which a SPECIES is distributed

**Receptive** when a female is ready to mate (in ESTRUS)

**Reproduction** the process of breeding, creating new offspring for the next generation

**Retina** light-sensitive layer at the back of the eye

**Retractile** capable of being withdrawn, as in claws of typical cats, which can be folded back into the paws to protect them from damage when walking

**Riparian** living beside rivers and lakes

**Roadkill** animals killed by road traffic

**Rumen** complex stomach found in RUMINANTS specifically for digesting plant material

**Ruminant** animals that eat vegetation and later bring it back from the stomach to chew again ("chewing the cud" or "rumination") to assist its digestion by microbes in the stomach

**Savanna** tropical grasslands with scattered trees and low rainfall, usually in warm areas

**Scats** fecal pellets, especially of CARNIVORES. SCENT is often deposited with the pellets as territorial markers

**Scent** chemicals produced by animals to leave smell messages for others to find and interpret

**Scrotum** bag of skin in which the male testicles are located

**Scrub** vegetation dominated by shrubs—woody plants usually with more than one stem

**Secondary forest** trees that have been planted or grown up on cleared ground

**Siblings** brothers and sisters

**Social behavior** interactions between individuals within the same SPECIES, e.g., courtship

**Species** a group of animals that look similar and can breed to produce fertile offspring

**Sub-Saharan** all parts of Africa lying south of the Sahara Desert

**Subspecies** a locally distinct group of animals that differ slightly from normal appearance of SPECIES; often called a race

**Symbiosis** when two or more SPECIES live together for their mutual benefit, more successfully than either could live on its own

**Syndactylous** fingers or toes that are joined along their length into a single structure

**Taxonomy** the branch of biology concerned with classifying ORGANISMS into groups according to similarities in their structure, origins, or behavior. The categories, in order of increasing broadness, are: SPECIES, GENUS, FAMILY, ORDER, class, and phylum. See Volume 1 page 11

**Terrestrial** living on land

**Territory** defended space

**Thermoregulation** the maintenance of a relatively constant body temperature either by adjustments to METABOLISM or by moving between sunshine and shade

**Torpor** deep sleep accompanied by lowered body temperature and reduced METABOLIC RATE

**Translocation** transferring members of a SPECIES from one location to another

**Underfur** fine hairs forming a dense, woolly mass close to the skin and underneath the outer coat of stiff hairs in mammals

**Ungulate** hoofed animals such as pigs, deer, cattle, and horses; mostly HERBIVORES

**Uterus** womb in which embryos of mammals develop

**Ultrasounds** sounds that are too high-pitched for humans to hear

**Ungulate** hoofed animal

**Ventral** the belly or underneath of an animal (opposite of DORSAL)

**Vertebrate** animal with a backbone (e.g., fish, mammals, reptiles), usually with a skeleton made of bones, but sometimes softer cartilage

**Vibrissae** sensory whiskers, usually on snout, but can be on areas such as elbows, tail, and eyebrows

**Viviparous** animals that give birth to active young rather than laying eggs

**Vocalization** making of sounds such as barking and croaking

**Zoologist** person who studies animals

**Zoology** the study of animals

# Further Reading

## General

Eisenberg, J. F., and Redford, K. H., **The Mammals of the Neotropics**, University of Chicago Press, Chicago, IL, 1999

King, C. M., **The Handbook of New Zealand Mammals**, Oxford University Press, Oxford, U.K., 1995

MacDonald, D., **Collins Field Guide to the Mammals of Britain and Europe**, Harper Collins, New York, NY, 1993

MacDonald, D., **The Encyclopedia of Mammals**, Barnes and Noble, New York, NY, 2001

Nowak, R. M., **Walker's Mammals of the World**, The John Hopkins University Press, Baltimore, MD, 1999

Strahan, R., **The Mammals of Australia**, Reed New Holland, Australia, 1998

Whitaker, J. O., **National Audubon Society Field Guide to North American Mammals**, Alfred A., Knopf, New York, NY, 1996

Wilson, D. E., **The Smithsonian Book of North American Mammals**, Smithsonian Institution Press, Washington, DC, 1999

Wilson, D. E., and Reeder, D.M., **Mammal Species of the World. A Taxonomic and Geographic Reference**, Smithsonian Institution Pres, Washington, DC, 1999

Young, J. Z., **The Life of Mammals: Their Anatomy and Physiology**, Oxford University Press, Oxford, U.K., 1975

## Specific to this volume

Bailey, C., **Tiger Tales: Stories of the Tasmanian Tiger**, Angus and Robertson, ??, U.K., 2001

Flannery, T., **Possums of the World**, Geo Publications, Chatswood, Australia, 1994

Grant, T., **The Platypus**, New South Wales University Press, Australia, 1984

Kerle, A., **Possums: The Brushtails, Ringtails, and Greater Glider**, University of New South Wales Press, Australia, 2001

Paddle, R., **The Last Tasmanian Tiger**, Cambridge University Press, U.K., 2000

# Useful Websites

## General

http://animaldiversity.ummz.umich.edu/
University of Michigan Museum of Zoology animal diversity websites. Search for pictures and information about animals by class, family, and common name. Includes glossary

http://www.cites.org/
IUCN and CITES listings. Search for animals by scientific name, order, family, genus, species, or common name. Location by country and explanation of reasons for listings

http://endangered.fws.gov
Information about threatened animals and plants from the U.S. Fish and Wildlife Service, the organization in charge of 94 million acres (38 million ha) of American wildlife refuges

http://www.iucn.org
Details of species and their status listings by the International Union for the Conservation of Nature, also lists IUCN publications

http://www.ewt.org.za
Website for threatened South African wildlife

http://www.panda.org
World Wide Fund for Nature (WWF), newsroom, press releases, government reports, campaigns

http://www.aza.org
American Zoo and Aquarium Association

http://www.ultimateungulate.com
Guide to world's hoofed mammals

http://www.wcs.org
Website of the Wildlife Conservation Society

http://www.nwf.org
Website of the National Wildlife Federation

http://www.nmnh.si.edu/msw/
Mammals list on Smithsonian Museum site

http://www.press.jhu.edu/books/walkers_mammals_of_the_world/prep.html
Text of basic book listing species, illustrating almost every genus

## Specific to this volume

http://www.naturalworlds.org/thylacine/index.htm
The thylacine (virtual) museum

http://www.savethekoala.com/
The Koala Foundation, information about koalas and their conservation
http://www.nccnsw.org.au
Website for threatened Australian species

http://www.ozramp.net.au/~senani/kangaroo.htm
All about kangaroos in words and pictures
http://www.noahsark.org.au/kangfire.htm
Discussion of the conservation status of kangaroos, the animal's use for meat, etc.

www.red-kangaroos.com/
Information on the red kangaroo with pictures and links

http://www.museumofhoaxes.com/platypus.html
Information about the platypus

http://www.wildlife-australia.com/platypus1.htm
Another source of information about the platypus

http://www.ozramp.net.au/~senani/echidna.htm
Information about echidnas, with links

# Set Index

A **bold** number shows the volume and is followed by the relevant page numbers (e.g., **1**: 52, 74).

Common names in **bold** (e.g., **aardwolf**) mean that the animal has an illustrated main entry in the set. Underlined page numbers (e.g., **9**: 78–79) refer to the main entry for that animal.

Italic page numbers (e.g., **2**: 103) point to illustrations of animals in parts of the set other than the main entry.

Page numbers in parentheses—e.g., **1**: (24)—locate information in At-a-Glance boxes.

Animals that get main entries in the set are indexed under their common names, alternative common names, and scientific names.

# Picture Credits

## Abbreviations

| | |
|---|---|
| A | Ardea |
| FLPA | Frank Lane Picture Agency |
| NHPA | Natural History Photographic Agency |
| NPL | naturepl.com |
| OSF | Oxford Scientific Films |
| SPP | Steve Parish Publishing |

t = top; b = bottom; c = center; l = left; r = right

## Jacket

tl caracal, Pete Oxford/naturepl.com; tr group of dolphins, Robert Harding Picture Library; bl lowland gorilla, Martin Rügner/Naturphotographie; br Rothchild's giraffe, Gerard Lacz/FLPA

**8–9** Dave Watts/NHPA; **10** John Cancalosi/Bruce Coleman Collection; **12–13** Konrad Wothe/OSF; **15** G.I. Bernard/NHPA; **18–19** T. Kitchen & V. Hurst/NHPA; **20** Lynda Richardson/Corbis; **21t** Rod Planck/NHPA; **21b** Alan & Sandy Carey/OSF; **22–23** Jack Dermid/OSF; **26** Jean-Paul Ferrero/A; **28–29** SPP; **30–31** Karen Gowlett-Holmes/OSF; **31** SPP; **32–33** Jean-Paul Ferrero/A; **34–35** A.G. (Bert) Wells/OSF; **36–37** Dave Watts; **38–39** A.N.T./NHPA; **40–41** Jean-Paul Ferrero/A; **42–43** M.W. Gillam/A; **44–45, 46–47** A.N.T./NHPA; **49** Martin Harvey/NHPA; **51** Kathie Atkinson/OSF; **53** Bruce Burkhardt/Corbis; **54–55** C. Andrew Henley/LARUS; **57t** Jean-Paul Ferrero/A; **57b** SPP; **58–59** Gallo Images/Corbis; **60–61** SPP; **62** Jean-Paul Ferrero/A; **62–63** C. Andrew Henley/LARUS; **64–65** Dave Watts; **66–67** Daniel J. Cox/OSF; **68–69** Eric Woods/OSF; **70–71** SPP; **72–73, 75** Dave Watts/NHPA; **77** Hans & Judy Beste/A; **78–79** SPP; **79** C. Andrew Henley/LARUS; **80–81** Peter Reese/NPL; **81** Dave Watts; **82–83** Jean-Paul Ferrero/A; **84–85** C. Andrew Henley/LARUS; **86–87** A.N.T./NHPA; **88–89** Jean-Paul Ferrero/A; **90–91** Pavel German/NHPA; **92–93** C. Andrew Henley/LARUS; **94, 95l** SPP; **95r** Gerard Lacz/NHPA; **96–97** Jim Frazier/Mantis Wildlife Films/OSF; **98–99** SPP; **100–101** Dave Watts/NHPA; **101** John Cancalosi/NPL; **102–103** Babs & Bert Wells/OSF; **104–105** D. Parer & E. Parer-Cook/A; **105b** M. McKelvey & P. Rismiller; **106–107** Hans & Judy Beste/A; **108** Dave Watts/NHPA; **108–109, 110–111** Dave Watts

# Artists

Denys Ovenden, Priscilla Barrett with Michael Long, Graham Allen, Malcolm McGregor

*While every effort has been made to trace the copyright holders of illustrations reproduced in this book, the publishers will be pleased to rectify any omissions or inaccuracies.*